PROFIT FIRST

FOR

REAL ESTATE INVESTING

PROFIT FIRST

FIRST

FOR

REAL ESTATE INVESTING

DAVID RICHTER

ISBN (paperback): 978-1-7375148-1-7
ISBN (ebook): 978-1-7375148-0-0

Disclaimer:
The information contained within this book is for informational purposes only. It should not be considered financial, legal, or tax advice. You should seek the services of an attorney or tax professional to determine what may be best for your individual needs.

Page Design & Typesetting: Chinook Design, Inc. (chinooktype.com)
Copy Editor: Zoë Bird

CONTENTS

I dedicate this book to you, the reader, real estate investor, and entrepreneur who wants to transform your business and life and never worry about money again.

FOREWORD

Books change lives. The author puts all their knowledge of their particular area of expertise into a few hundred pages. It's printed, digitized to an e-reader format, or recorded to an audio file. And voilà, the reader has a cheat sheet to achieving their goal. Years, decades, or even a lifetime of knowledge is collected, collated, compressed, and packaged up. The best of the best resides right there in your hands.

I am convinced you are about to experience the same with this book. David Richter is about to transform your life. I know it because he has put that transformational power within these pages. A lifetime of knowledge is in these pages. Your job is simple: Read it and do it.

David's own life was transformed through a book too. He read *Rich Dad Poor Dad* by Robert Kiyosaki. As he dug into the pages, it inspired him to become a real estate investor. He bought his first house, fixed it up, and lease optioned the property. The tenant cashed him out six months later. Transformed by the book, David devoted his career to real estate investing. His thirst for knowledge grew. His desire to share what he learned grew.

While doing personal deals as a side hustle, David joined a small real estate investing company with seven people who closed just under ninety deals a year. He helped grow the company to become one with thirty employees who closed three hundred deals a year. David guided the business through flips, wholesales, turnkeys, rentals, lease options, creative financing, and a variety of exit strategies. But that was just the beginning.

David has served in every capacity you can within the real estate investing realm. He has facilitated marketing, sales, property acquisition, property management, project management, transaction coordination, and financing. He knows the process inside and out. And he knows the challenges inside and out too. The biggest problem? Cash flow management. And David knows how to fix it.

David was quickly recruited by another real estate investor to transform their finances. Through simple and impactful enhancements to their cash management process, he was able to immediately transform the investor's business.

In 2019, David launched Simple CFO Solutions to help real estate investors make more money and keep more money. His method? Profit First. Specifically, Profit First enhanced for real estate investors. Within a year, Simple CFO Solutions has already served seventy-seven real estate entities to enhance their financial acuity. David made them more money and helped them keep more money. He saved them from the struggles that riddle the industry.

I wonder if you can relate. Have you experienced the highs and lows (as in really low lows) of living deal to deal? Have you experienced cash surging in and inevitably surging out? Do you feel that everyone else in the industry has it "dialed in" and you don't? Would you rather ignore your finances than try to sort out the tangled mess? Are you not paying yourself enough? Consistently? Or even at all? If you said yes to even one of these questions, I have good news. You are not alone and there is a solution. And if you said yes to many or all of these questions, your situation is very fixable. This book answers every question and more.

How do I know? Because of David's track record. He makes real estate investors profitable, every single time. He took the Profit First principles and enhanced them specifically for your needs. He extracted the best of the best financial strategies from the hundreds of transactions he has facilitated and the countless other ones he has studied. He has distilled the lessons of some of the greatest investors of all time. And he has packed it all in this book for you.

After implementing what David teaches within these pages, one investor said to David, "If I had started this system years ago, I would have five million more in my bank account today." Heed that thought. You too can have five million or more sitting in your bank account. But for that to happen, you need to start the system today. Immediate action will bring long-term wealth. Waiting a moment too long will simply prolong your financial struggle. Read this book *and* do this book.

David has your solution, but there is one more thing you should know before you get started. He cares. He loves the industry, and he loves the people in it. He knows that real estate is a force for good. It brings wealth and security to countless people. It affords quality homes for people who otherwise would not have access. And it is one of the biggest components of our global economy.

Your success is everyone's success. David and I want that for you. And you can have it. You simply have to take the next steps. Start reading. Start doing.

I can't think of a better deal on this planet—real estate included—than reading a book that transforms your life. A book that was written by an industry authority, for your industry, to fix your biggest need. You have it in front of you right now, in this moment. So get started, right now, in this moment. Your life is about to be transformed by this book.

Mike Michalowicz, author of *Profit First*

INTRODUCTION

"The only thing that money gives you is the freedom of not worrying about money."
Johnny Carson

He hung up on me!
He hung up on me?
Yep, he hung up on me.

I sat stunned in my chair. A thousand different thoughts raced through my head. *Did I say something wrong? Was Dan mad at me? Is this the end of our relationship?* I got up from my chair and paced around my office because I thought I had hurt my client.

Before I tell you why Dan Guerin hung up on me, let me tell you a little bit about him. He's a man's man. This guy is seven feet tall—at least that's how I feel standing next to him, but I'm short, so that applies to most people. He's fought for our freedoms; he served in the military, where he earned a Purple Heart. He fought on the front line in places like Baghdad, Mosul, and Tal Afar. He's had a job processing disconnects for a cable company. (I imagine breaking people's thumbs like Rocky Balboa's first job, but probably not.) He goes skydiving, blows up more fireworks than your local government on the Fourth of July, and lives life to the absolute fullest. He is married with four kids, so you know this guy has to be tough. And, just like you, he owns his own real estate investing company.

When Dan got out of the army, he had several different jobs. He worked in construction and he installed commercial swimming pools. He started real estate investing on the side while he enjoyed the W-2 job and the pay. He helped grow the pool installation company from about $320,000 in annual revenue to about $2.1 million. He received an annual bonus each December on the sales he made. Not too shabby.

Then it happened: That same year his efforts took the pool installation company to $2.1 million annual revenue, Dan's bosses called him into a meeting.

"We changed the structure of the bonuses," one of them said. "You will receive about half of what was expected. We had to use a different accounting method, so our hands are tied."

Dan looked them both in the eye and told them, "I took this company from hundreds of thousands in sales to millions. With those excuses for why you won't pay what is owed, then you've helped me decide whether or not to move on. I'm done with both of you and this company."

This was Dan's *Jerry McGuire* moment.

Just like that, Dan became a full-time real estate investor.

And, just like that, he had an aversion to any mention of accounting or finance.

Like so many investors, when Dan first got into real estate, he thought he just had to do deals and the money would take care of itself. That approach changed his life dramatically. When he left his job, he didn't have any debt. Fast forward two years into his real estate investing journey, he was in a lot of debt and worried about going out of business. The finances he didn't want to think about were slowly killing him.

This larger-than-life man who had seen live combat, received the Purple Heart, and had four kids had one major fear: his finances. Worries about all the debt piling up and how to keep the company afloat kept him up at night. He didn't know where he stood financially in his company and that lack of knowledge brought even more fear. He knew he probably wasn't on the right track, but he didn't know his numbers, and when he tried to understand them, he became confused. All that uncertainty brought another level of stress.

Dan eventually went to the deepest, darkest place and thought, *I have a great life insurance policy that would take care of my wife and children for the rest of their lives and clear all the debt. I want to make sure my family would be taken care of no matter what. Maybe this is the answer to my problems?*

When those thoughts entered his head, he knew he needed help.

I met Dan in a real estate mastermind group. He reached out to me, and we started working together. In a matter of a few weeks, we rehabbed the numbers so we could see the picture of where his company stood. Then came the fateful call—I had to tell Dan his company's financial story, and it wasn't good news.

Feeling a little sick to my stomach, I launched the Zoom meeting. As Dan and his right-hand man, Jake, logged in, my heart beat faster.

I began walking them through the numbers. "Your operating expenses are about 85% of the gross profit for the year and after taking your owner's draws, Dan, your company's net profit is negative."

No one said a word. I started to sweat.

Then Dan said, "This is ridiculous."

He ended the Zoom call.

Dan later told me that, after he hung up, he got up and raced out his office building. "I paced back and forth, feeling so embarrassed. I felt like a total failure and hated having to show Jake where we stood. I wondered why I was in this business."

You are a real estate investor. Maybe the fear and worry Dan had about his finances resonates with you. Perhaps, like him, you're up at night worrying about your company and its cash. How does not knowing your company finances make you feel? Maybe you're scared if you look at the numbers, you won't like what you see. Maybe you have dark thoughts and wonder if it would be easier to give up on everything and cash in your life for the insurance policy.

Maybe you've tried to figure out the financial side but haven't found anything that has stuck. So you went out, hired the first bookkeeper or CPA you could find, washed your hands of the finances, left it all in their hands, and still nothing got any better or more clear.

Or maybe you don't have a lot of stress around your finances. Maybe you don't think about it much. Maybe you are frugal and don't have a lot of expenses, but still struggle to know the best way to grow your business. You might say to yourself, *I'll figure out my finances one day.*

"One day" can sneak up on you.

And even if you're sure "one day" will never come, that you won't end up like Dan, what about lost opportunity? Not knowing your numbers can keep you from achieving goals and dreams.

I started in real estate after reading—wait for it—*Rich Dad Poor Dad,* during college. It completely changed my views on finances and gave me a passion for real estate. After consuming that book and about fifty others on real estate as fast as I possibly could, I went out and bought my first deal because I needed to buy a deal instead of just reading about it. I bought a foreclosed property, so I'd have instant equity. I fixed the house up and then lived in it for two years. Upon moving out, I lease optioned that property. The tenant I put in the house was Super

Tenant. He paid early every month and then six months into his agreement, he bought the house and cashed me out. I was so excited about that deal! I had the real estate investing bug and knew I had to do more.

After that first property, I sought out other real estate investors in the area where I lived in northwest Indiana. I eventually came on board with someone who had a team of about seven people; they did about seven wholesale deals a month. In that company, I got a massive hands-on business education. I sat in every single seat. I ran acquisitions, dispositions (selling the properties), project management of rehabs, property management of rentals, transaction coordination, marketing, and accounting. We took that company from closing seven deals a month to twenty-five to thirty deals a month. We did all kinds of exit strategies at that point too. We wholesaled, wholetailed (light rehab then sell retail), retailed, rented, lease optioned, owner financed, and basically every exit strategy under the sun. We also grew our team from about seven people to about thirty. In the time I was there, I was a part of more than eight hundred deals, including ones I did myself.

Sitting in the accounting seat made me realize how important it is to know where your company stands financially. Our CPA taught me how to keep the books. I asked him questions such as, "Why does this transaction go here? If I assign this transaction to this account, where does it end up on the financial reports?"

After asking about a million of those questions, I started to understand how telling the numbers were. The numbers seemed way out of whack. We had so much in overhead. At the time, payroll was over 50% of expenses, when a healthy company should be around 30%. Red lights and warning bells went off in my head.

Then it hit me: It didn't matter how many deals we did, because we ran negative almost every month. We needed to increase revenue right away or make a major cut in expenses.

The company had to scale way back, so I made a life change. After selling my properties in Northwest Indiana, I moved with my wife and daughter near Richmond, Virginia, and began to work with another real estate investor in the area. His issues with finances were similar to the last company I worked for, and with the knowledge and experience I'd gained, I helped him turn his finances around. I'll share his story later in the book, but I bring it up now because seeing the peace and confidence this transformation gave him inspired me to think about how I might help other real estate investors turn their own finances around.

And when he looked me straight in the eyes and told me, "You've changed my life," I knew at that moment that I had a new bug. I wanted to change the lives of real estate investors everywhere. *Someone* had to help them; someone had to make finances simple and easy to understand, so I answered that calling.

I started my company, Simple CFO Solutions, to help real estate investors gain financial clarity and freedom through knowing their numbers.

I knew I could make a difference, but I was a little nervous about taking the leap. So I called respected people in the industry with whom I had built relationships over the years and told them my mission.

I remember calling Gary Harper, a good friend and mentor of mine. I sat on the edge of my bathtub and shared my idea, and my fears.

I'll never forget what Gary said: "You have a duty and responsibility to help as many investors as possible and to do everything in your power to make it happen."

This was the push I needed that started the domino effect that eventually became this book.

During one of the conversations I had with Gary, he told me I should read the book *Profit First* by Mike Michalowicz because that would help me with the business I started. As soon as we hung up the phone, I bought the book on Audible and consumed it that evening. I took ten pages of notes.

Reading *Profit First* changed my life. This book was the "aha" moment for me that took a tired cliché I'd heard before—"pay yourself first"—and backed it up with action steps. I *knew* this system would help real estate investors stop living deal to deal. *Profit First* finally put into words the financial system I knew the real estate world needed to stop missing out on profit they already made. This system and book has changed the lives of countless business owners and entrepreneurs, and I wanted countless real estate investors' lives to be changed too.

In talking with several hundred real estate investors, I'd say that over 95% of them do not have any true system set up for their finances. They may have a great CPA or great bookkeeper, which are still very few and far between, but they do not have a repeatable system to manage their cash and make sure they get the maximum benefits from the business.

I wrote this book because after implementing Profit First in real estate investing businesses with my Simple CFO Solutions business and seeing the results and the lives changed, I knew I had to get the Profit First message to *all* real estate investors. I can't serve every investor (*yet* *wink wink*), but I knew there had to be a book specifically for them.

For you.

I want *your* life to change the same way my clients' lives have changed. I truly believe if you take the actions outlined in this book you will gain the financial clarity you need to keep the profit you've *already earned* and stop living deal to deal.

And Dan Guerin? Well, thankfully, he didn't stay mad and upset too long after he hung up on me at that fateful meeting. We were able to reconnect later that day.

He called and told me, "Hey, Dave, I'm sorry for hanging up earlier. I was embarrassed because the numbers are so bad, and Jake heard how bad our company is doing. But I am ready to change. I am ready to not be stressed anymore about money. I'm ready to get the burden off my back of feeling like I'm drowning in debt. I'm tired of not sleeping. I am trusting you and the process to get us where we need to be."

I let out a breath I hadn't realized I'd been holding. "Dan, I understand that talking about the numbers has been tough to hear, but I'm glad you've decided to take control back. You have the knowledge and power now to make that change. Let's make it happen."

I care about Dan, and I care about you. I want to tell you right out of the gate that I believe in you and care about you. If you are reading this, you are my people. I believe in you as a real estate investor. I believe in you as a person. You are worth more to the world than sleepless nights and living in fear about your finances. I care deeply that you stop having fights with your significant other over finances. I care about stopping the pain of letting down your family. I care about stopping the guilt of not being able to provide the life you promised your family. I care about stopping the feelings of being a fraud when you are around other investors and pretending that everything is okay. I care about stopping the business from going belly up and stopping the pain of seeing your business fold up along with the hopes and dreams you had for that business. I care about helping you achieve all of your goals and dreams.

This book can help you. This book can help you calm the fears, stop the guilt, heal the pain, put the power back in your hands, and help you achieve true financial freedom. I wrote this book for *you*.

One of my favorite movies is *Forrest Gump*. There is such a great part that deals with finances. It's after Forrest and Lieutenant Dan started Bubba Gump Shrimp Company and are making good money. Lieutenant Dan mails a letter to Forrest and tells him that he invested their money in "some sort of fruit company," which turns out to be Apple. Forrest sits on the iconic bench with the chocolates in his lap telling a stranger this story and says, "Lieutenant Dan got me invested in some kind of fruit company. So then I got a call from him, saying we don't have to worry about money no more. And I said, 'That's good! One less thing.'"

That's what I want this book to be for you. After reading this book and implementing its principles, I want you to sit back and say that you don't have to worry about money anymore, so that's one less thing. This book can do that for you.

Chapter 1

WHY YOU'RE LIVING
DEAL TO DEAL

"I am the problem."

Sitting next to my wife, Angela, in the counselor's office, the light finally turned on in my brain. The constructs I had created in my head about faith, family, and finances, were built on what someone told me and not on what I discovered for myself.

My wife and I have been married for seven years as of the writing of this book. This past year was one of the most difficult for us. We've had health scares. Our daughter had to have surgery, and the medical bills were astronomical. Family issues we swept under the rug for the past seven years began rearing their ugly head, and we took our internal issues out on each other. We chose to get counseling because we didn't want to continue in the same way.

This is not a marriage counseling book, but I want you to know I have the same challenges everyone has, and I also had to realize I contributed to the problem. I sought out a counselor and came to him with a very open mind and heart because I wanted to change. I wanted things to be better in our marriage. My wife wanted the same thing too, thankfully.

In one session, we talked in-depth about finances. Finances have always been a sore subject between us. I am the epitome of a saver, and she is the epitome of a spender. I always thought I was the one in the right because I wanted to save and plan and invest, while I always felt she wanted to just spend every dollar.

I remember the session on finances like it was yesterday.

"Tell me about the problems you face around finances," the counselor began.

"My husband is so uptight and every conversation we have I feel like he wants to restrict us spending. I want to enjoy life now," Angela said.

"I agree I'm uptight about the finances, but she spends so much I feel like I have to be, or we will eventually have nothing if we keep running at this rate," I replied.

Angela responded, "I don't spend much more than we need, and there's always more available."

"I want to be able to take advantage of opportunities that come up and I want to make sure we are building wealth and not just spending every dollar," I explained. "I want to save so we can get into a new house, invest in the business, invest in real estate, go on vacation, and so on."

The counselor asked me one question. "Have you ever talked with Angela about these things and why you want them?"

Oh shoot, I thought. "Nope, I've never really given her an explanation. I always talk about being on the same page, but I never made it a priority."

Turns out that after that session and talking with my wife that we both wanted the same things. We both wanted to live a good life today and capitalize on the opportunities of tomorrow. We just weren't on the same page.

I don't care if you identify as a saver, spender, or investor: You need to realize that some of the ideas you have about money are flat out wrong. I also hope you come to this book with an open mind, willing to let go of preconceived notions about money and investments. In this book I will teach you different strategies and tactics to make sure you ultimately grow your wealth and receive the full benefits from your business, and those strategies and tactics may require you to let go of those preconceived notions.

Angela and I had more sessions with the counselor. He listened, absorbed, and diagnosed. And you know what? Turns out a lot of my life I had been living to please others and have them like me instead of saying what needed to be said. Thankfully, I've learned to absorb feedback and implement it right away, so our marriage got a lot better in a short amount of time and has stayed better.

Why do I tell you this very personal story? For several reasons:

1. Despite all of the personal development I'd done up until that point, my mindset was wrong, and I needed a guide to help me see that.
2. I want to help you understand that the formula section below and the process of implementing Profit First for Real Estate Investing (PFREI) will require a change in mindset around money.
3. Lastly, I want you to realize that you have a guide in this book.

In these pages you have someone who has listened to hundreds of real estate investors over the last ten years talk about their financial fears, absorbed those fears, and now wants to guide you to a solution. I had to face the way I thought and realize some thoughts I had were wrong. I want to help you figure out where you may need to think differently about your finances. The real investors profiled in the stories in this book have taken the steps to become the business owners we all aspire to be. I hope you learn from them too. I do not want you to live deal to deal, and there is help in this book to stop that vicious cycle.

THE REAL ESTATE RAT RACE

Will my card go through? Bob thought as his wife happily shopped in Nordstrom for Christmas presents for their family. As soon as they walked into the store, a sharp pain had pierced his stomach and stayed with him as his wife picked out shirts, purses, clothes, and other accessories. When it came time to check out, sweat poured down his back. Would his credit card be declined?

Bob walked up to the register feeling as though he was about to pass out, handed the cashier his card, and held his breath.

This time, the charge was approved. He exhaled and tried to hide his relief.

Bob wholesaled houses and made money, but every time he pulled out a credit card to pay for something he could never be sure if the transaction would go through. Even though he actively closed deals consistently, he had no idea where he stood with his finances. He lived like so many investors. At masterminds, he'd puff out his chest and talk about how many deals he'd done, but he knew he didn't have money in his account. He looked sparkling clean on the outside but felt like a dirty dishrag on the inside. He hated himself for being a fraud. Stuck in the rat race, Bob lived deal to deal and wondered which one would be the last before he had to close up shop.

At some point or another, you probably read *Rich Dad Poor Dad* by Robert Kiyosaki. I reference his book several times, so I suggest reading it if you haven't. If you have read it, and you really enjoyed it, you may have also played Kiyosaki's board game,

Cashflow 101. The whole point of the board game is to get out of the rat race, which is a reference to a life in which you get up, go to work, trade your time for money, and then repeat this loop forever.

No matter what, you got into real estate because at some level, even if you haven't read *Rich Dad Poor Dad,* you wanted to get out of the rat race.

This was one reason I invested in real estate. The idea of working every day and doing the same thing over and over again really depressed me. The whole idea of the rat race still makes me want to shudder and cry in a corner. I got into real estate to escape all of that, and that was one reason if not *the* reason you jumped into real estate too.

Let's talk about where you are now. Do you work fifty, sixty, seventy, eighty hours or more a week in your real estate company and just spin your wheels? Perhaps you dread every single phone call because it may be another contractor, tenant, or seller to waste your time, or another problem you have to focus on. Maybe you live deal to deal and day to day. Have you paid yourself consistently this year?

Where's the financial freedom everyone talks about? Where is the money that is supposed to pour in from your deals and let you live the life you've always wanted to live?

Didn't you get started in real estate to *escape* the rat race?

In reality, so many of us trade one rat race for another.

The Real Estate Rat Race drags you down and makes you want to quit and give up. You're more stressed financially than ever. You work more hours than you ever have. You run full speed all the time but just can't seem to get ahead. You have a ton of money in your bank account one day and the very next day you run on "E." You hate the up-down vicious cycle of having money, not having money; getting deals, scrambling for deals; the phone ringing off the hook, the phone silent as the grave.

The Real Estate Rat Race is real. It's something early investors struggle with constantly. Even seasoned investors can get bogged down in it. I've talked with new investors and investors closing over one hundred deals a year, and both groups feel the *exact* same way. You are *not* alone in feeling like you spin in circles and think that there has to be a better way to make money. I felt this way too.

I hope you're reading this book because you've realized real estate investing is more than just making the deals happen. It's about keeping the money from the deals too.

WHY DID YOU START YOUR BUSINESS?

I want you to be real with yourself and ask yourself some tough questions. When you think about your company, what kind of emotion do you feel? Pride? Happiness? Stress? Anger? Confusion? Out of control? Is your business profitable? Do you pay yourself what you need to feed your family? Do you love real estate and hunting deals, but hate a part of your business because it seems like you spin your wheels for no reason?

You are not alone. I've talked to hundreds of real estate investors during my journey of writing this book, and literally 99% of them said there was a point in time that they were not paying themselves consistently. They drew money at random times and let their personal finances get out of hand. They didn't take money out of the business because they wanted to "reinvest" as much as possible back into the business. Everyone I talked to also said that this was an incredibly stressful time in their lives.

For the first two years of his real estate business, Dan, the investor you met in the introduction, took draws from the company when he thought he could because he didn't know where he stood financially. It was super stressful not to have a set amount he knew he could draw safely, and he never, ever wanted to be in that position again. Dan and Bob and so many of the investors I work with said, "Enough! We will pay ourselves what we need to because we started our businesses to make a positive difference in our lives and not to lose sleep and be stressed month after month."

As a fellow real estate investor and business owner, I understand wanting to pour every dime you earn into the business. I get wanting to self-fund and use every penny to get the business rolling. But if you are past the startup phase and closing five or more deals a year, then you should pay yourself consistently. I'm not saying you should pay yourself a ridiculous salary; pay yourself what you need. You didn't start the business just to feed the business and to limp along beside it while it ate all your money.

There is a way out of the real estate rat race. You *can* pay yourself first.

THE FORMULA THAT CHANGES EVERYTHING

What I'm about to share with you will change your life. I know that's a bold statement, but I'm confident in making it because I've seen it happen over and over again.

If you've read *Profit First* by Mike Michalowicz, you know that most accountants follow this standard formula for calculating profit:

SALES – EXPENSES = PROFIT

That formula seems pretty logical, doesn't it? And that is probably how you run your business right now. You sell a property or collect rent, and then you pay everyone and your mother before you pay yourself and take whatever might be leftover at the end of the day. And yet this whole mindset and the actions behind it actually are a slap in the face to every book you've read that says to pay yourself first!

When you read the books that advocated paying yourself first, I'm sure you were super-pumped and ready to get started. You dove into real estate and started closing deals. Then came the first few hires because you needed help.

Then came the systems and software. Pretty soon you had so many expenses you *had* to do deals because your costs ran wild.

You are no longer in control of your business, and it has become a cash-eating monster. You wake up every day knowing that your expenses eat you alive, and the cash in your business is always in a precarious situation. The "pay yourself first" principle is completely out the window because you can't let everyone down. In fact, you may be taking home *less* pay than you did before you got into real estate investing, just to ensure you can cover all of your expenses. You think the answer is getting more deals or better profit deals. And yet, no matter how many deals you close or how profitable they are, you still struggle with cash flow.

The solution is not more deals. The solution is fixing the formula.

The reason I love the *Profit First* approach to calculating profit is that it flips the formula on its head and makes one subtle but significant change:

SALES – PROFIT = EXPENSES

This formula is transformational because it shifts you from thinking about your expenses first and puts you and the health of your company first. When the deals roll in, profit is the first money that should be allocated. You might be thinking, "Yeah right! You can't make it that simple! I have too many expenses or can't set aside profit first." And I'd say you're right if you have that mentality. If you think that way, Profit First has already uncovered a big problem for you, and that problem will eventually kill your business. That cash-eating monster is never satisfied, and the rat race will never end. If you have the mindset that you can't take your profit first, then you owe it to yourself, your family, your employees, your future, and everyone around you to change your thinking. It isn't your fault that you weren't taught this formula until now. It will be your fault if you don't make a change after learning the life-changing principles in the rest of this book.

THE PROMISE OF PROFIT FIRST

"Every single month there was a pain point brought up with my business partner because we didn't pay ourselves consistently or much of anything from our real estate business. Even when we made more money, we poured the extra cash into the business, which ultimately hurt us and caused sleepless nights." This is what Ben Fredricks told me his life was like before implementing Profit First.

When Ben first started in real estate, he lived deal to deal. As is true for most investors, he jumped into business without much knowledge of knowing how to handle the money from the business. He also had a business partner who shared in the struggle. The stress of the business was multiplied because if they weren't doing well, two people suffered. I mention the business partner because Ben told me before implementing Profit First inside of his real estate business, the number one reason he lost sleep was that his business partner was always super stressed and vocalized it constantly. They met monthly to discuss the finances, and every time, his partner expressed his concerns about the lack of consistent pay.

Then, Ben and his business partner started closing more deals and making more money, and they were surprised their real estate business took off like it did. This brought another stressful situation to the company: They received a huge tax bill from Uncle Sam.

Ben told me, "When we received that tax bill, the pain came over me in waves. I felt the pounding in my head and a sharp pain in the pit of my stomach. Not only had we not been paying ourselves consistently, we also had not been saving for our taxes, so we felt out of control."

Thankfully, Ben knew he needed mentoring and guidance in his business and had already joined a mastermind to help the business grow. He shared in his mastermind the struggles he and his partner had with cash flow, paying themselves, and the stress from the tax bill they received. Several people in the mastermind had read *Profit First* and pointed him to that book.

Ben told me, "This was the turning point for my business."

He got the book and devoured its pages and started implementing the Profit First system within two weeks of reading the book. He trusted the system and knew anything other than what they had been doing would be worth trying.

Ben fell in love with the system right away. "When you haven't had any system and are just running the business off what knowledge you might have about finances and then you actually implement a proven system to manage the money, it's life-changing."

Ben plowed through the upfront process of opening the bank accounts and started allocating the income as it came into his **Profit** account first. He put himself and his business partner on payroll and started collecting consistent paychecks. They had finally realized the goal of getting themselves paid.

"There was no sense of loss from paying ourselves," Ben told me, "but a sense of feeling that isn't this what the business was always supposed to do for us? Weren't we supposed to gain from our hard work?" They had put in a lot of time and energy into their business, and it paid off by gaining knowledge and taking action. They were now managing their money instead of their money managing them.

"About two months into paying ourselves, this is when it hit me that the system truly worked," Ben explained. "My business partner was not stressed, and it had been several months since the sleepless nights for either of us because my partner is being paid consistently, and we steadily saved for our taxes."

Ben's story is consistent with a lot of investors that I've worked with or interviewed who have implemented Profit First. This was the beginning of a major change in the way they thought about themselves: from real estate investor to business owner.

REAL ESTATE INVESTOR VERSUS BUSINESS OWNER

As real estate investors, we are pulled in many different directions. One day we might have to be a marketer, or an acquisitions manager, or do follow-up, or sell the deals, or God forbid, do the bookkeeping and financial management.

Making a mental shift from real estate investor to business owner will help you maximize the contents of this book. A real estate investor cares about the next deal. A business owner cares about every aspect of the business. A business owner knows he needs the right mindset, the best people in the appropriate seats, the best systems in place, and the key financial knowledge to get the maximum profit from his company.

Right now, it may seem out of reach to imagine not doing everything yourself, but I want you to start moving in that direction. The first step is implementing Profit First in your business.

Real Estate Investor	Business Owner
Pulls lists, designs letters/postcards, sets up campaigns, mails the campaigns, and so on.	Has a marketing team or manager
Takes all phone calls	Has a lead manager to take phone calls
Goes out on every appointment	Has an acquisitions manager to run appointments
Doesn't follow up or is inconsistent	Has a killer *automated* follow-up system in place
Messes with paperwork and title issues	Has a transaction coordinator that handles all paperwork and title issues
Personally sells all the deals himself	Has a dispositions manager to sell the deals
Goes out to every project	Has a project manager
Takes calls from tenants at ungodly hours, yells at late tenants, cries in a corner	Has a property manager
Doesn't know the numbers or keep track of books	Has a PFREI bookkeeper in place, knows the numbers, and keeps up to date weekly
Doesn't pay himself because he's "reinvesting" everything into his business	Pays herself first and makes sure she's healthy
Doesn't know where all the money is and lives deal to deal	Runs on Profit First

After you've done that, you can start making other important shifts, like the ones in the table above.

I get that at the beginning of your real estate investing journey, you will sit on the real estate investor side of this chart until you are profitable enough to outsource those responsibilities. You may or may not want a big team. No matter what, as the business owner, you will need to learn how to handle the finances. You must figure out enough on the financial side of your business to make sure you are able to keep your company healthy.

According to the Small Business Administration, more than 85% of business owners do not know how to read a financial statement. After working in this business for the last decade, I'd push that percentage even higher and say 95% of real estate investors do not know how to manage money in general. Do you see that if you run your business finances with your head in the sand that you are in the majority of investors? Do you want to be in this majority?

Being a real estate investor already means you're different than most people. Maybe you always had the entrepreneurial bug, but you worked for someone else and finally made that commitment to yourself and went out and started your own real estate investing company. *Different.* Or maybe you worked a W-2 job and knew that you needed to stop working for "the man," and quit to start investing. *Different.*

Take that same passion and energy you felt when you started your real estate company and turn it on yourself and say, "No more!" No more will you be unprofitable. *Different.* No more will you close deals and let money slip through your fingers. *Different.* No more will you rack up expenses so high that you can't pay yourself or have any money for profit. *Different.* No more will you live deal to deal and paycheck to paycheck like so many other real estate investors. *Different.* No more will you just be a real estate investor: Commit to being a business owner. *Different.* You will be *different.*

You have big goals and dreams. You want financial freedom, to retire early, to take your family on amazing trips, to give back to your community, or to change the world in some way. If you are constantly stressed about your finances and living deal to deal, you will not be able to focus on why you started your company. Just as Bob was so worried about his card going through that he couldn't enjoy spending time with his wife, you will not be able to enjoy the little moments of happiness or fulfill your life's mission if you are always worried about where you stand financially. By the way, Bob is now a multimillionaire and has a successful business where he maximizes his owner's benefit. He doesn't have to worry about his card being declined any more.

Profit unlocks your "why." It turbocharges your goals and dreams. When you become permanently profitable by internalizing the formula, shifting your mindset, and taking your profit first, you will be on the path to accomplishing why you began real estate investing.

This is the true purpose behind PFREI (Profit First REI). This system isn't about setting up bank accounts or making transfers. It's about giving you the benefits you always desired as a business owner and giving you the best life possible.

You're living deal to deal because you need someone to guide you to permanent profitability. You will learn in the next few pages how to stay profitable forever.

START NOW

If you are ready to transform, please take action right now. As in right this second. The real estate investors who truly want to be different than the rest of the pack are defined by the actions they take. This one step is an important one for you to commit to me and to yourself that you are ready to be a business owner and take responsibility for your finances. Email me right now at pfreibook@simplecfosolutions.com with the initials "PF REI" in the subject line and the words "I am ready to stop living deal to deal" in the email. You will get a response confirming I'm on this journey with you.

Chapter 2

PAY YOURSELF
FIRST—FOR REAL

"All wealth is based on systems."
Dan Kennedy

Picture yourself in a race. You get to the starting line without any preparation, and you realize that you have no idea where the finish line is. You think, *Oh well, I'll just follow the crowd.* You start running and you think this is supposed to be a short race but all the other people run for one mile, then two, then three, and you think, *What in the world type of race did I join?* You think about quitting because you have no idea what the goal of the race is. You have no idea how to measure your progress. You have no clear direction, no preparation, and no end goal in sight. You hit some speed bumps along the way and that makes you fall out of the race because you don't know when the race will end or even the point of the race.

How frustrating would that be to you? That would drive me absolutely insane. Isn't this how most of us as real estate investors run our businesses? We have no clear end goal of what true financial freedom means to us. We haven't sat down to think what the end looks like. Then we sell properties and buy rentals, but with no clear goal, we spin our wheels and get frustrated with our business. I've been there. I feel your pain. When I was in my early twenties and bought my own rentals, I used the cash flow for expenses, saving, investing, or whatever dog barked loudest. When I started my own business, I didn't have a clear goal of where I wanted to take it at the beginning. I quickly realized though that I did not want to live every day as an owner not knowing where I wanted to end. Even though I read *Profit First* and had implemented it in my business, I still needed guidance. I taught this system, but I knew I needed someone to hold me accountable and help clarify my goals. I hired a part-time CFO (Chief Financial Officer) for our own business to hold me to my financial goals. It took serious focus, but clarifying where I wanted to be helped make all other decisions easier.

As I talked about in Chapter 1, a *lot* of the other books you've read as a real estate investor pound into your head that you should pay yourself first. I agree with them 100%. The difference in this book is that I want to give you an actual process and system to pay yourself first. I want to help you define what your end goal should be and give you action steps to follow.

In this chapter, I'll go over the Profit First for Real Estate Investing system in brief, and then I'll cover each of those steps in detail in the next few chapters. But before we get into the system, you first need to figure out your finish line. What do you need and what do you want? When I work with clients, the first step is to have an owner's compensation meeting. I'll walk you through that process in this chapter. Let's dive in.

TWO CRUCIAL NUMBERS

When you've completed this next exercise, I want you to write down two numbers: how much you Need to earn and how much you Want to make. The Need number is the most important right now because it will help determine the Want number. Since your business is an extension of who you are, you need to pay yourself what you *need*.

As business owners we rely on our businesses and our businesses rely on us. I am going to get personal with you, and you need to get real with yourself. Your personal finances, whether you like it or not, affect your business finances. You live deal to deal because you aren't able to pay yourself enough (or anything!) from each deal to feel like your business is truly supporting you, so you need to take a hard look at your personal finances. I am all about making sure you not only have enough to cover your expenses but also live a lifestyle that you love and enjoy. The first step, though, is to get into a healthy position.

How do you calculate the number you need every month to cover your expenses? If you don't have fancy software or a spreadsheet or anything already tracking your personal finances, I'd suggest printing out your personal bank and credit card statements for the last two quarters. Then, add up what you spent for the last six months and then divide it by six to get the average of what you spend in a month. If you've never done this before, then the number will probably shock you. You now have several questions to ask yourself:

1. Is that number a realistic number that you need to support yourself and your lifestyle?
2. If not, how much do I need?
3. Can my business realistically support this number? (We'll cover this in the next section.)

After answering these three questions, you should have your Need number. Now I want you to find the Want number. I'll make it very simple for you. Take your Need number and multiply it by at least two. Your Want number should excite you and let you live how you want, so if double your Need number doesn't cut it for you, then triple it, or quadruple it. Like I said, you want the Want number to excite you!

> **How to get the Need number:** Need = Personal bank and credit card statements for the last six months and the average of what you spent.

> **Example:** You spent $42,000 for the last six months. Your Need number would be $42,000 *divided by* six to give you monthly personal expenses of $7,000 per month.

$42,000	÷	6	=	$7,000
(AMOUNT SPENT IN 2 QUARTERS)		(NUMBER OF MONTHS)		(AVERAGE MONTHLY PERSONAL EXPENSES)

> **How to get the Want number:** Want = Need number *times* (at least) two.

> **Example:** Take the $7,000 that you found as your Need number and multiply it by two.

$7,000	×	2	=	$14,000
(NEED NUMBER)		(MULTIPLIER)		(WANT NUMBER)

Does that number excite you? Keep it. If it doesn't, multiply the Need number by three and so on.

Here's a tip: You can delegate the task of finding the Need number to someone on your team or hire a virtual assistant to go through your statements, but remember to block out any account numbers or information. Tell them exactly what you are looking for and be clear.

Now that you have your numbers, let's see if your business can really support you.

CAN YOUR BUSINESS SUPPORT YOUR NEEDS AND WANTS?

Take what you made over the last twelve months in your business and see what percentage of what you're making in the business you would need to pay yourself. How do you do this? Remember the Need number that you just calculated? We need the annual Need number to see how much you need to pay yourself in a year. Take your monthly Need number and multiply it by twelve. Real complicated math, I know. In our example we had $7,000 as the monthly Need number. Multiplying $7,000 by twelve gives us $84,000 a year that you Need.

Now that you know that annual Need number, you will be able to calculate a whole host of other numbers in your business. The next number I want you to focus on is how many deals you need to do and at what profit point you need to do them in order to pay yourself what you Need. Let's say your business makes $240,000 in a year. A healthy percentage to pay yourself at this level of revenue is about 35% to 50%. If you do the math, $240,000 times 35% is $84,000. If your business makes $240,000 a year, you can pay yourself at least 35% of what you bring in based on the Need number ($84,000) we calculated together. If you can pay yourself 50%, you could be paying yourself $120,000, which would be closer to your Want number.

Do you see that by knowing what you *need* to make, you can project how many deals and how much each deal should average in profit to bring home what you need? Let's do an example.

If you are a fix-and-flipper who averages about $30,000 in profit per flip, how many flips would you need to do in a year to make sure you could pay yourself $84,000 and have that number be 35% of your business? Because we know we need $240,000 as a business goal to be able to pay ourselves 35% to give us $84,000, we can take $240,000 and divide that number by $30,000 in deal profitability to give us the number of deals in a year. In this case, it's eight deals a year or two deals per quarter in the year.

As investors, we love our formulas, so if these formulas didn't make sense, let me give you some clear-cut formulas you can plug numbers in to find out if a deal is really a *good* deal for you.

Formula 1: Find how much your business needs to make: your Need number *divided by* the percent you need to pay yourself *equals* your business goal.

Example:

$84,000	÷	35%	=	$240,000
(NEED NUMBER)		(PERCENT TO PAY YOURSELF)		(BUSINESS GOAL)

Formula 2: Find how many deals a year you need to do in order to hit your business goal: your business goal *divided by* your average profit per deal *equals* the number of deals you need to do in a year.

Examples:

$240,000	÷	$30,000	=	8
(BUSINESS GOAL)		(AVERAGE PROFIT PER DEAL)		(NUMBER OF DEALS IN A YEAR)

$240,000	÷	$3,600	=	66
(BUSINESS GOAL)		(AVERAGE CASH PER RENTAL IN A YEAR)		(RENTAL PORTFOLIO)

Do you see the power you have unlocked from knowing your Need number? No matter if you are in the wholesaling, renting, or flipping business, you can calculate what the business needs to bring in in order to support you.

As a part of this book, I've built a spreadsheet for you to be able to calculate these numbers for what you need. Go to simplecfosolutions.com/pfrei to find it.

Understanding your numbers is an important step in freeing yourself from living deal to deal and finally reaping the benefits of real estate investment. Take Joey English, for example. He is a real estate investor who took a vacation recently with money from his **Profit** account. He had to pay taxes for the first time in years because he made money in his companies, but he had exactly what he needed in his **Tax** account to pay them. It didn't start this way, though.

Joey has two companies: a rental portfolio along with a fix-and-flip business. His flipping business funded the expenses of both his companies, and he didn't pay himself anything from the sales of the houses. He hadn't paid himself from the fix-and-flip company in the five years he had been in business. He fixed up properties like a madman, spinning his wheels, and worked countless hours, just to pay other people.

He was more stressed than he had ever been in his life. He started gaining weight. Everything hurt all the time, he had high blood pressure, and felt more out of control than ever before. The flipping business drained him physically, emotionally, mentally, and drained his bank account.

On top of all of this, Joey's wife, Ashley, had to come into the business to help because there was so much work to do. She tried to be a good wife, mother, and business partner, but having to play the different roles brought a tremendous amount of stress. She started having seizures because of the toll that the business took on her.

Ashley told me this story after we worked together for a while. As they worked in the office, stacks of papers everywhere, she busily typed away on her keyboard, talked on the phone, and tried to eat a bite of her lunch, when she suddenly stopped, looked at Joey and said, "Joey, I feel so out of control. How do we get it back?"

Joey replied, "Honey, I'm doing the best I can, but we have to tough it out. It will get better but right now I have to go and look at a house."

She wondered, *Will this rat race ever end?*

But they hadn't reached the lowest point yet. Joey told me about a meeting with his accountant to go over his books at the end of the year.

The accountant said, "After looking at your books, if I ever thought about fix- and-flipping before, I sure wouldn't now. You lost over $70,000 this year." Joey felt like he had just been run over by a freight train.

He got cold sweats and had trouble driving home.

That night, after they got the kids to bed, he told his wife the news.

She sat stunned at how much they had lost, but she knew she needed to be strong for her husband. "Joey, we'll figure it out. We'll make it work. We will do better together." She silently prayed for her words to come true.

Joey tried to gain control back. He went to his bookkeeper and CPA to ask for help to know where he stood and to explain his books to him in a way he could understand, but because neither of them was a real estate investor, they would talk circles around him, and he'd end up more confused, frustrated, and feeling even more out of control.

Joey heard a story a long time ago about Arnold Schwarzenegger and how he had massive arms, but his stomach embarrassed him, so he would walk around with a cutoff shirt to show his stomach to everyone. This was Arnold's way of holding himself accountable to others. In one final effort to gain control back, get back on the right path, and hold himself accountable, Joey told everyone at his different real estate groups and masterminds how he had lost $70,000 and how out of control he felt. People recommended Joey talk to me because they thought I could guide him back to the light. After hearing me present at an event we both attended together, he decided to talk to me.

When Joey and I first had a conversation, I knew that even though he had a lost a lot of money, we could help him. He is an amazing person in general and loves real estate. He is a very giving human being. I was very motivated to help and guide him.

When I first started working with Joey, he told me, "I hate fixing and flipping." He had thought the harder he worked and the more deals he did, the more money he would make. At the end of the year when his accountant told him he lost $70,000, he knew working extra hard and more deals weren't the answer. He knew he needed help gaining control back over his business and having the business work for him instead of always feeding the monster.

Because I am a real estate investor, I knew how to talk to Joey and because of the framework of our system, I knew we'd be able to help him right away. His books were relatively clean (I say "relatively" because some people have come to us with six years' worth of clean-up and Joey's was nothing like that), so I was able to explain financial basics and teach him how to read the financial statements. Being able to read the statements was a light bulb moment for him. He could now look at his books and know exactly how much he was into a property (such as purchase price *plus* all rehab costs) and that gave him a lot of control over knowing where he stood budget-wise on his fix-and-flip properties.

The core of Profit First for Real Estate Investing is to make sure the owner reaps the benefits of starting the business. Teaching that every decision needs to be made with profitability in mind helped change Joey's mindset from more deals to more profitable deals and maybe fewer deals done overall in a year. He saw the light that his flip company needed to pay him if he did any of the work inside of that company.

Joey had a vision of helping fund a camp for kids, but that mission had been on the back burner while he tried to keep his head above water. Needless to say, if the business is losing money, it's hard to fulfill the reasons behind starting the business. He needed to stop feeling stressed and out of control in order to be profitable and fulfill his mission.

We walked Joey through the steps to make sure his business made enough to pay him what he needed. We had to get him to the point where he felt comfortable paying himself and not using his flipping business as just a money pit.

Just as we walked Joey through the steps of PFREI, I want to give you the overview of the steps and then dive into them in depth in the next couple chapters.

Let's get to what you care about: The steps of PFREI.

STEP ONE: RUN THE PFREI INSTANT ASSESSMENT

In order to improve, you need a baseline. It's hard to say you're more profitable this year than last if you don't have some way to assess that information. The instant assessment is a *very* simple and easy way to gain this knowledge. You only need to know two numbers: your income and what you paid yourself in the last twelve months. You can work every number needed from there. You don't have to have a clean set of books or any books or financial records set up to run this assessment. We ran one with Joey to know what he paid himself and what he made. This gave us a baseline, and from there, we could find ways to make improvements. This was eye-opening for Joey because it revealed his fix-and-flip company funneled a lot of money away from his rental business and didn't provide any value at all to him. This is why he hated fixing and flipping, but now he had a way to quantify that sentiment.

STEP TWO: SET UP YOUR ACCOUNTS

I know you. I know what you do right now with your bank account. You look at the one main account and it's the gauge for whether you go into panic mode or whether you feel like a million bucks. When you have money in it, you're happy. When you don't have money in it, you feel extreme stress.

This is even worse for you as a real estate investor because that one bank account holds all of your funds and other people's money. You know if that account gets low, you have not only spent your money, but have also spent the private money you borrowed for properties.

If you have heard of the envelope method of handling your finances, you can relate to this step. This is about setting up new bank accounts to separate the money into "buckets" that hold your cash for specific reasons. These should be business bank accounts tied to one of your entities. You will run your core business from these new accounts. These new accounts bring major clarity to your business because at a glance you can see what you have to spend on certain areas in your business. This step helped Joey separate the money for the business and gain insight on the health and cash position of the business, something he had never had before.

I still love the foundational accounts from *Profit First* because of the instant clarity separating your money gives you. The foundational accounts are:

1. **Income:** This is a holding bucket for your money until you transfer the income to the other accounts.
2. **Profit:** This is the foundational account that will help you become and stay profitable.
3. **Owner's Comp:** This account ensures you pay yourself for the work you do in the business.
4. **Owner's Tax:** This account is for saving for the taxes you pay Uncle Sam throughout the year. As the owner, your business should pay your taxes for you.
5. **OpEx (Operating Expense):** You already have this account set up because you already pay bills and operational expenses.

6. **OPM (Other People's Money):** This account will save your bacon because it's for the money received from private lenders for your rehabs. I'll go into this account more in depth in the next chapter.

I also propose that real estate investors set up another account right away called **Reserves**. If you do not want to worry about your finances or whether a not a property closed, add a **Reserves** account right from the start to give yourself breathing room.

These bank accounts make sure you have a profit, and that you can pay yourself, save for taxes, and have enough money to run the business. I suggest calling your bank and starting the process to set them up right away.

You might think, "Six or seven accounts? That seems like overkill!"

Let me ask you, is your current money management system working for you? Does it bring you less stress and more clarity? If setting up all the accounts seems overwhelming, set up one new account and name it **Profit**. Start where *you* can. The only way to fail at this system is by not doing anything. You have permission to do what works for *you*. Set up one new account dedicated to the profitability of your company and transfer 1% of all sales into that account. Start small and where you can if you don't set up all the accounts at one time. This will put you on the path to permanent profitability.

Joey originally balked at the idea of all the accounts. He now has ten different bank accounts. He told me recently, "I don't know how I ever lived without the clarity all ten provide me. I'm never going back to one account."

STEP THREE: THE REAL ESTATE RHYTHM

Anything in life worth accomplishing requires discipline. This step is about the rhythm and habit of transfers into the new accounts when income is deposited. I am very excited to get into this step because it guides you to make an inconsistent business as consistent as possible for you. I will tell about what to do if you have infrequent sales or very frequent sales, and making transfers if you have rentals. Joey is a great example again because he had fix-and-flips and rentals, and the transfers are handled differently for both types of properties.

After you start this step, you will control your finances instead of your finances controlling you. Gone are the haphazard days of thinking about your money inconsistently and not being on top of where you are financially.

THE REASON PFREI WORKS

One of the biggest benefits of the Profit First for Real Estate Investing system is that it works with your current behavior. Sometime today you probably checked your bank account just to get a pulse of your finances. That isn't the clearest picture of your finances currently, but it lets you know whether you should panic or not.

PFREI leverages your current habits and behaviors such as checking your bank accounts to give you clarity. What if you looked at your bank accounts and could see right away whether you have enough money to hire another team member or that you have true profit saved for whatever you want?

One of the many other reasons PFREI works is it forces you to take your profit first. It instills in you the need to be a healthy company and not grow at all costs. Most real estate investors, myself included, get caught up with the shiny object syndrome and want to invest in any opportunity that crosses our paths. Sometimes the best opportunities are the ones we never take. PFREI helps you view them from the standpoint of profitability and the health of your company. This system can help you filter deals to make sure they align with the overall health of your business.

STOP WORRYING ABOUT MONEY!

Everyone worries about money, right? You may worry about your finances every day, once a week, or once a month. I want this book to put you in the position to never worry about money again. For Dan, the investor who hung up on me, fears about finances kept him up at night. For Joey, profit was inconsistent and sometimes nonexistent, and finances confused him. As I'm writing this book, both Joey and Dan have told me almost the exact same thing: "I don't have to worry about money anymore because of the systems, the reserves, and the mindset given to me through our Profit First journey."

Earlier I talked about why PFREI works, but I created this whole section separately because I think addressing your fears and doubts is the biggest reason the system succeeds. It gives you a new way to think about finances that helps you achieve a sense of peace and security that will last a lifetime.

STOP COMPARING YOURSELF TO OTHERS

One of the main reasons Joey lost $70,000 was that he fell into the trap of comparing himself to others. He would go to masterminds and hear in the room how someone was "scaling up" their business and closing five, ten, fifteen, and twenty deals a month, and he'd talk down to himself and think that he should be doing more deals. This is one driving force that fueled his downward spiral as a fix-and-flipper. He thought he needed to scale up his business after he came back from these places. This brought a tremendous amount of stress and anxiety to him and his family. It affected every area of his life. He knew something had to change. Thankfully, as we worked together, he made the decision to scale back his business and work on what he really needed from his fix-and-flip company to be healthy.

As an investor, you might go to masterminds and meetups and hear about other people doing an insane number of deals, or you might close an insane amount of deals yourself. The question I want you to ask yourself is, *Do I close these deals because I want to or because it's what I think others want me to do or think I should do?* If it's because you want to, you enjoy it, and you're able to pay yourself, please keep doing those deals. If you kill yourself every day and run in the real estate rat race and live deal to deal, please take a hard look at where you are now, and take some time to look inside yourself and figure out what you want from your business. Then you can plan what *your* company should look like and not what someone else thinks your company should be.

Bigger isn't better. Better is better. You can do the same amount of deals or even fewer deals and make and keep more money than you are currently making. That's the whole point of this book.

PFREI IS A TEAM EFFORT

We've all been there. Can you think back to high school (scary, I know) and remember when you were assigned a group project? There was always the person in the group who wanted to get the "A" on the project and would take over if they had to. This was completely me. There were always the people who didn't do anything. Then you had the clueless ones who never knew what went on but "tried" helping. Unless the school project was something everyone in the group loved with a passion, everyone wasn't really on board and some felt like they had better things to do. If you were ever lucky enough to get all your friends to work on a project, besides having a lot of fun, you probably worked better with them because of your common bond. You were able to get the project done and with less stress because if you all wanted to make it happen, you worked on a common goal with people you trusted.

The PFREI system is really a team effort. To be successful with the system, you need to make sure that everyone who works with you and the people who work on the financial side of your business are on board with the system. I want to bring to your attention the people on your team that you need to help you succeed and hold you accountable. Do not keep Profit First to yourself. Shout it from the rooftops that you are implementing the system and then come down from the roof and tell your people. Who exactly do you need to tell?

1. Talk to your CPA, bookkeeper, or financial team about the system.

    This is a big one. Your CPA and bookkeeper, if they have never heard of the Profit First system, will have a lot of questions and probably be skeptical at first. THIS IS TOTALLY NORMAL AND OKAY. Give them a copy of this book and tell them to read it and give it a chance. Then tell them this is how you will run your finances and ask them if they will be on board with it.

You can give them a couple days to read the book, but don't wait to begin the system.

If the CPA or bookkeeper doesn't want to run the system, you need to find a new CPA or bookkeeper.

2. Talk to your team about PFREI.

This is more for a morale boost than anything else. Tell them you will take ownership over the finances and implement a system to manage them. This will give your team peace of mind. You should always look for ways to bring assurance to your team and show them that you lead by example.

The PFREI system can also help you with managing payroll and bonuses too, and making sure you have enough money to pay people. This system puts a lot of power back in your hands instead of conceding power at every turn. This will give you more confidence with your team and in yourself.

Another item you might want to consider sharing with your team is the actual percentages and the tactics of PFREI. You might say that you don't want people knowing what the business makes or what your Owner's Comp is, and I get it. Up to this point, you probably haven't shared anything like that with the team but that's probably been more out of just not knowing than fearing how knowing those numbers would affect them. Your team members already think you're a queen or king making all the dough all the time. It would be good to give them a dose of reality and let them know that every dollar that comes in has a place to go and a percentage tied to it. Even if you make six, seven, or eight figures a month, you know more than anyone that a lot of those dollars are spoken for by expenses, taxes, and investments that the business makes.

Consider telling your team that your top line revenue is just that, top line, and that the money gets divided up to pay their salary, the tax man, and to make sure the business and you as the owner are healthy financially. This will give them a dose of reality because even though it seems you make a lot, every dollar is spoken for and not all of the income goes straight into your pocket.

3. If you have a business partner, make sure they are on board.

If your partner doesn't understand why you opened up bank accounts or the point of the system, give them this book as a guide to help them understand. Tell them the point of the system is to help your business be as healthy and profitable as possible and give clarity in the finances. If your partner is not on board, send them to the PFREI podcast to hear all the real estate owners who have implemented Profit First and the success stories they have to tell. If—after you've given them this book, explained why you want to implement the system for the health and profitability of the business, and they've listened to some success stories of from other investors—they still don't want to implement the system, you might want to take a long, hard look at your relationship.

If you don't have a business partner, tell your spouse your plan. Joey's wife was the one who told him to take a chance on working with my team and me and setting up PFREI in their business. Because you will take the time to invest in your business and yourself by implementing this system, give your spouse peace of mind by sharing your journey.

SECURE YOUR DREAM

Spoiler Alert: Joey's story does have a happy ending. After realizing he needed to stop comparing himself to other investors and what he thought was expected of a real estate investor, we helped him plan out exactly what he Needed to pay himself from his flipping company. After implementing the PFREI system, Joey's fix-and-flip business now covers his Needs and his rental business covers his Wants. He pays himself from his flipping company and doesn't worry about the cash flow dips because he has evened out the cash by using the Profit First system and allocating his funds into the different accounts every time he has a sale.

He told me, "One of the biggest benefits I get from using PFREI is that I think in quarters and years now and not just deal-to-deal profitability. I used to think that as long as the deals were profitable, I was okay, but after working with you, I realized that the deals can be profitable but the company can be sick if it eats all of the deals' profitability."

He stopped trying to close more deals and focused on more profitable deals. Able to pay himself what he needs from his flipping entity, he now uses the funds he paid himself in his rental business to lower the good debt on his houses which generates more cash every month and have free and clear properties in his portfolio. He can meet his ultimate goal of funding a camp for children, which is why he started his businesses. He recently paid off a mortgage, and it added $1,000 a month to his cash flow that he uses to pay down the mortgages on other houses. He is on track to have a free and clear portfolio in three to four years. The snowball effect is in full force. This is the power of the system.

Joey saves for taxes throughout the year now too. He called me at the end of 2020 after working together for about a year and told me, "I met with my accountant again. Needless to say she was a lot more tempted to get into fixing and flipping because she told me I made a lot of money this year. She also told me I'd have to pay taxes. David, I haven't had to pay taxes for years because I didn't make money in my flipping company. I'm excited that I get to pay taxes because it represents that I made money! She then gave me an estimate of what I would owe in taxes. While I was on the phone with her, I looked at my tax accounts and I already had her estimate saved! This system works!"

Being able to pay himself, pay down his debt, know his numbers, and save for taxes freed Joey from the real estate rat race and gave him back his life.

He told me, "I feel better than I've felt in a long time. I have worked out consistently every morning. I run two to three 5ks a week. My overall health and happiness are greater because of the freedom that PFREI has provided. I've done less deals and am more profitable than ever. I am in control of my numbers instead of them controlling me. We recently took a vacation that we paid in full from our **Profit** account. We also set aside a percentage to give to the camp. This system has changed my life and will change the lives of those children I've always wanted to help."

Joey is well on his way to funding the camp and will have more than five figures worth of savings to donate directly to his dream in less than a year.

I also asked Joey's wife, Ashley, how she feels now. She said, "I don't have to be in the business anymore. I can focus on being the wife and mother I need to be for my family. My stress levels are way down, and I finally feel in control instead of spinning in circles. Our lives have completely changed. I feel hopeful for the future and have hope in PFREI and never want Joey to stop the system. Thank you for helping us get our lives back."

Now I want to picture yourself in a race again. Only this time, you've spent time preparing, planning, and know exactly where the finish line is. You have the right equipment and gear to get you the full length of the race and you know when you need to rest and take a break. You get to the starting line, and you feel a thousand times better and know that you can get where you want to go. During the race you hit some speed bumps, but are able to course correct and stay on track because you keep that end goal in sight and have prepared for bumps along the way. You start passing milestone markers and celebrate the little wins during your journey. You get to the finish line and people pat you on the back. You then go out the next day and start planning for another race because you have the power to make those decisions and take the actions you know you need to take in order to run and finish.

You can be just like Joey. You *can* pay yourself first. You *can* get on track to fund the big goals and dreams you have for your business. You *can* get control back. You *can* live the life you were meant to live. You *can* do the same number of deals and put more money in your pocket right now. You *deserve* to have a business that supports you and creates your financial freedom.

START NOW

To show you are committed to stop living deal to deal, I want you to take action right now. Open one new bank account and transfer 1% of all property profit or rental income into that account. This will put you on the path to make profit a habit in your real estate investing company. Start where you can. This is a great place to do something besides just reading. If you can't make this happen, you may not want to read the rest of the book because there are more practical action steps to take in the following chapters.

Thank you for sticking with me this far. The next few chapters are all action steps based on the steps of Profit First and how to implement the system fully into your business, so you can start making more money without more headache or the stress of trying to get a ton more deals.

Chapter 3

STEP ONE: THE PFREI INSTANT ASSESSMENT

I had it all wrong. When I first implemented Profit First in my own business, I mistakenly thought that I had to have a complete set of financial records and my books had to be completely clean and up to date. This could not be further from the truth when you begin your PFREI journey.

Most real estate investors give their accountants a shoebox full of receipts, a spreadsheet, or a set of incomplete books during tax time and say, "Here, fix this, and get me a tax return." That is the extent of their financials. If you don't have a clean set of books, you will still close deals and bring in cash. You will never say, "Let me stop my deal flow to fix my books." I get it completely, which is why I want to help change the behavior of buying properties without a plan for your cash no matter whether your books are clean or not. Like I said, you will never stop closing deals, so you still need a system to manage your cash no matter what.

If you didn't read the introduction, you missed out on the story of Dan Guerin, the real estate investor who hung up on me on one of our first calls together. He hung up on me because we ran an instant assessment for him, and the outcome was a hard pill to swallow. However, this basic understanding of where he stood financially was *the* turning point for Dan. He now had data to tell him where he was, so he could improve drastically from that point. The assessment helped change his behavior. He could hold himself financially accountable because he now had a baseline.

I want you to know where you stand right now so you can begin to enjoy the benefits of your business. Just as Joey was able to take his family on vacations from his **Profit** account and pay down his portfolio to fund a camp for children, it all started with taking stock of his current situation.

To perform the PFREI Instant Assessment on your business, you only need to know two numbers: how much you made in Real Revenue and how much you put in your pocket in the last twelve months. You do not need a complete set of financials or to have your books completely up to date as I mistakenly thought when I first implemented the system.

Let's get to what you care about: the steps to run the instant assessment.

FIND OUT WHAT YOU MADE (REAL REVENUE)

Finding out what you made in the last six to twelve months is the first step to run the instant assessment. You may have this number readily available, or you may need some time to get this as accurate as possible. The bottom line is that you need the Real Revenue from your business and *not* just the cash you received from the closings. "Real Revenue" is a term coined by Mike Michalowicz in *Profit First*. Put simply, this is how much true income you made in your business. This number is super important because a lot of other numbers we will figure out together depend on knowing the Real Revenue.

Another key term coined in *Profit First* is "Materials and Subcontractors." This category of expenses is anything that must be paid in order to contribute to the Real Revenue. For Profit First for Real Estate Investing, I've coined the term "Pass Through Revenue" instead of Materials and Subcontractors because real estate businesses have a lot of different expenses that flow right through the business before the actual Real Revenue is made. An example of Pass Through Revenue for real estate investors would be the "all-in" cost to sell a house, which would include the purchase price, the rehab amount, the holding costs, the closing costs, and any interest paid to a lender at closing. Pass Through Revenue would also be commissions you pay to sales reps when a property closes. To make any money, that rep had to do the work and get a signed contract; therefore, part of the revenue "passes through" to them. I would also say the principal, interest, taxes, and insurance (PITI) on your rental properties would be considered Pass Through Revenue because you must pay the principal, interest, taxes, and insurance to keep the property.

Let's break down the Real Revenue for a selling company versus a rental or creative financing business.

FORMULA TO FIND REAL REVENUE FOR A SELLING COMPANY

Selling Company Definition: Whenever I use the term "selling company", I mean any type of exit strategy that involves selling the house such as wholesale double closings, assignment of contracts, wholetails, fix-and-flips, turnkeys, and so on.

On the selling side, to find the Real Revenue number is very simple: Take the sale price of your property *minus* any costs associated with that property from when you purchase until you sell it. If you just assign contracts, your Real Revenue number is the assignment fee *minus* any costs, if any at all, associated with that property.

> **Formula:** Sale Price *minus* Pass Through Revenue (purchase price *plus* rehab *plus* closing and holding costs) *equals* Real Revenue

Example:

	$100,000	(SALE PRICE)
−	$50,000	(PURCHASE PRICE)
−	$25,000	(REHAB)
−	$5,000	(CLOSING AND HOLDING COSTS)
=	$20,000	REAL REVENUE

For the sake of the instant assessment, if you have a spreadsheet or some software that tells you what you think the profit is from each deal you did in the last twelve months, add your profit per deal numbers to give you your Real Revenue for the last year. Please do not stress if you don't think you counted every single penny. If you sold twenty deals in the last twelve months, and you know you averaged $10,000 per deal, use $200,000 as the Real Revenue for the year.

The goal here is to give you a picture of where you've been without relying on your bookkeeper or anyone else to get you these numbers. If you have a great set of books, by all means use the property profit numbers that your bookkeeper can provide as the Real Revenue.

FORMULA TO FIND REAL REVENUE
FOR A RENTAL COMPANY

Rental Company Definition: Whenever I use the term "rental company" I mean any type of exit strategy where you potentially hold the property long-term (more than a year) such as rentals, lease options, land contracts, subject to deals, and so on.

You cannot look at the profit and loss statement for a rental company to get your business's whole story because any principal payments applied to mortgages sit on the balance sheet. That is actual cash out the door, so you need to know where you stand each month in Real Revenue.

For a rental business, your Real Revenue number is calculated by taking the rental income or creative financing income total *minus* the PITI on those properties. This gives you a real understanding of the actual cash that you have to work with in a month.

> **Formula:** Rental Income *plus* Owner Finance Income *minus* Pass Through Revenue (PITI) *equals* Real Revenue

Example:

	$10,000	(RENTAL/OWNER FINANCE INCOME)
−	$7,000	(PITI)
=	$3,000	(REAL REVENUE)

Finding the Real Revenue has been eye-opening to the buy and hold investors we work with, *especially* after their portfolio grew to more than a few rentals.

Again, don't stress if you can't figure out to the penny what your Real Revenue is for the last twelve months inside your rental company. Take your total rental income for the last twelve months and subtract the total mortgage and interest payments you've made on the rental portfolio.

If you read *Profit First* and couldn't figure out Real Revenue in your business, I hope that this section has clarified it for you. After working with many real estate investing companies, I can confidently say figuring out Real Revenue this way is the best way to know how much money you have to allocate and transfer to your Profit First accounts.

FIND HOW MUCH YOU KEPT

The next step is to find how much revenue you kept in the last twelve months, which should be relatively easy. If you have a great set of financial records, look at how much you took out of the business that directly benefited you. Did you take a salary? Count it. Did you take any owner's draws? Count it. Did you pay any other personal expenses that only relate to you from your business? Count it. If you don't have a great set of financial records, another way to find how much you kept is to look at your personal bank statements for the last six to twelve months and add up the deposits made from your business into your personal account and count that as how much you kept.

Again, I want this to be as simple as possible for you. If looking at your bank and credit card statements to try and find the personal expenses your business covered makes you want to tear your hair out, just move on and go with your Need number.

I talked with an investor recently and she told me, "I have no idea what I bring home because I use my business account to pay credit cards that I use for personal and business expenses. It would be a nightmare to find what I kept from my business."

I asked her, "Do you know how much you need from your business?"

"Yes, I recently went through everything that I spend in my personal life."

"Great! Use that number as your baseline of what you need to bring home and what you kept."

If you already use Profit First in your business and have accounts specifically dedicated to save for profit and your taxes, those numbers can be kept separate from the owner's compensation you took in the last year.

If you have multiple owners in the business, you need to add up any money kept by each owner to get your total. After you have that number, you are ready to run the instant assessment.

RUN THE INSTANT ASSESSMENT

Now that you know how much you made and kept from your business, you can identify how much of your Real Revenue you allocate to pay yourself, cover taxes, run your business, and so on. These numbers are your Current Allocation Percentages, or CAPs. For example, let's say your Real Revenue is $100,000 for the year. In this fictitious scenario (see the sample table on the next page), say you paid yourself $20,000 for the year but didn't set aside anything for taxes or profit. Your starting CAPs would be 0% Profit, 20% Owner's Comp, 0% Taxes, and 80% Operating Expenses.

I will teach you how to do a full-blown assessment in Chapter 7. For now, let's get a quick assessment of where you stand right now using the blank table on the next page or your own spreadsheet. I've also provided a template for the instant assessment here: simplecfosolutions.com/pfrei with built-in formulas to help you figure your CAPs. Jot down what you made in the box in the "Real Revenue" column. If you didn't save anything in a **Profit** account, put $0 in the profit row

SAMPLE INSTANT ASSESSMENT		
	CAPs	Amounts
Real Revenue		$100,000
Profit	0%	$0
Owner's Comp	20%	$20,000
Owner's Tax	0%	$0
Operating Expenses	80%	$80,000

YOUR INSTANT ASSESSMENT		
	CAPs	Amounts
Real Revenue		$_____
Profit	_____%	$_____
Owner's Comp	_____%	$_____
Owner's Tax	_____%	$_____
Operating Expenses	_____%	$_____

underneath the Actual $ column. Whatever amount you kept from your business, put that number in the Owner's Comp row. If you didn't save anything for your taxes in a separate account last year, put zero in the Owner's Tax row. In the Operating Expense row, you'll put the Real Revenue *minus* the Profit, Owner's Comp, and Owner's Tax numbers unless you know exactly how much you spent in the last twelve months. Again, this is to give you a rough idea of your CAPs. We will dive deeper later in the book.

Now, divide these numbers by the Real Revenue number to get your CAPs. For example, if your Real Revenue is $100,000 and you kept $50,000, 50% would go in the CAPs column in the Owner's Comp row.

You now have your CAPs. This can be a sobering experience because you might have to face some hard truths. Maybe you are only just now realizing that you don't pay yourself enough or that your operating expense is too high. These numbers don't say whether you did well or badly. This is simply where you are right now. Now you have a baseline to improve and start to get the benefits from the business that you've always dreamed about.

BUSINESS BENEFIT GOALS: TARGET ALLOCATION PERCENTAGES (TAPS)

Now that you have where you are, let's set some business benefit goals: your Target Allocation Percentages (TAPs). These are the percentages of the Real Revenue you should aim for to have a healthy company and to unlock the true benefits of why you started investing. You will now have a goal to shoot for in your finances rather than spinning your wheels without gaining traction. Your TAPs represent time and money freedom, vacations with your family, mission trips, funding a camp for children, or anything that you dream or aspire to do.

In *Profit First*, Mike included Target Allocation Percentages (TAPs) of what business owners should pay themselves based on the size of their business. I've found that for flipping companies those TAPs are spot on. The table below shows TAP recommendations for a selling company.

SELLING COMPANY TAPS						
	A	B	C	D	E	F
Annual Real Revenue Range	$0-$250K	$250-$500K	$500K -$1M	$1M -$5M	$5M -$10M	$10M -$50M
Real Revenue	100%	100%	100%	100%	100%	100%
Profit	5%	10%	15%	10%	15%	20%
Owner's Pay	50%	35%	20%	10%	5%	0%
Owner's Tax	15%	15%	15%	15%	15%	15%
Operating Expenses	30%	40%	50%	65%	65%	65%

	A	B	C	D	E	F
RENTAL COMPANY TAPS						
Annual Real Revenue Range	$0–$250K	$250–$500K	$500K–$1M	$1M–$5M	$5M–$10M	$10M–$50M
Real Revenue	100%	100%	100%	100%	100%	100%
Profit	10%	15%	20%	15%	20%	25%
Owner's Pay	40%	30%	15%	10%	5%	0%
Owner's Tax	5%	5%	5%	5%	5%	5%
Operating Expenses	30%	35%	45%	55%	55%	55%
Repairs, Vacancy, Turnover	15%	15%	15%	15%	15%	15%

For rental companies, the TAPs are a little different, as the Rental Company TAPs table above shows.

You can see there is an added foundational account for saving for Repairs, Vacancy, and Turnover because those items will always be a part of your rental business. The Profit and Owner's Tax numbers are different too because you probably don't need to save 5% in taxes because of depreciation. (Disclaimer: I'm not a CPA—I'm just going by real-world experience.) We allocate more to the **Profit** account because you can use that to start paying down the debt on your rentals if that is a goal of yours or to celebrate your profitability.

Let's assume you cash flow $300 a door after PITI and you have fifty doors. That means you would have $15,000 a month in Real Revenue ($300 times fifty doors in a month). That number times twelve would give you $180,000 in Real Revenue for the year, which puts you in column A of the TAPs. So if you're a

RENTAL COMPANY SAMPLE ASSESSMENT		
	CAPs	Amounts
Real Revenue		$15,000
Profit	10%	$1,500
Owner's Comp	40%	$6,000
Owner's Tax	5%	$750
Operating Expenses	30%	$4,500
Repairs, Vacancy, Turnover	15%	$2,250

healthy business bringing in $15,000 a month in Real Revenue, you'd put 10% to Profit ($1,500), 40% to Owner's Comp ($6,000), 5% to Owner's Tax ($750), 30% to Operating Expenses ($4,500), and 15% to Repairs/Vacancy/Turnover ($2,250) in a month. Do you see the power this gives you?

Paying down the principal and interest on your mortgages gives you more Real Revenue to allocate. Some investors want free and clear properties, whereas others want them to always be leveraged. It really depends on who you are and what goals you have, but paying down the good debt on your properties puts more cash into your pocket without buying any more rentals.

TAPs are the percentage targets you will aim to hit, the goal to keep in front of you at all times. When you begin implementing PFREI, you need to start with your Current Allocation Percentages (CAPs). You will probably not be at the TAPs when you first start the Profit First system, which is *okay*. If your business has not been very healthy up to this point, you may not be able to put 5%, 10%, 15% in the **Profit** account right away. The point is to put *something* in each account, so you may have to start at a lesser percentage (.5%, 1%, 2%) for some accounts such as the **Profit** account and may need to start at a higher percentage (80%, 90%, and so on) for other accounts, such as the **Operating Expense** account. *Do not* feel bad for starting out with totally different percentages than the TAPs.

START NOW

You now have actionable steps to start the PFREI process. Here is what you should do right now to get on the right path:

1. Calculate what you made and kept for yourself in the last twelve months and figure out your CAPs as outlined previously.

2. Project what your Real Revenue will be over a year and determine your TAPs. This is so important to give you a goal to work toward.

3. Consider hiring a team to help guide you through the initial assessment process if you don't feel comfortable doing it yourself.

Chapter 4

STEP TWO: SET UP ACCOUNTS TO SAVE YOUR SANITY

"Profit First completely changed my business and life. The bank accounts are a lifesaver," Jamie Wooleson Burley told me. But that wasn't how she felt about this step when she first implemented it.

Jamie is a true go-giver. In his amazing book, *The Go-Giver*, Bob Burg explains that a "go-giver" is someone who adds value to everything and everyone they touch. Jamie started her real estate journey like most of us do. Disorganized, running from fire to fire, and riding the cash flow roller coaster of having money and then not having money, she lived deal to deal. She "reinvested" her profit back into her business by purchasing deals with the cash in her one bank account. That cash was really needed to cover expenses and payroll, but Jamie didn't know how to calculate when she'd need her cash.

Sometimes she'd take draws out of the business and feel guilty because she didn't know if that would hurt the company or if she could have used that money to invest in another property. She had never really been taught how to manage business finances or what to look for or how to analyze cash flow. She felt very disorganized and stressed when it came to her finances.

Jamie told me a story that changed her perspective. "I was at my friends' house, and saw they used the envelope method, which meant they separated money into different envelopes for certain areas of their finances like mortgage payments, groceries, giving, living expenses, savings, and so on. My initial thought was that this process was over the top. A system like that seemed constricting to me because they were limited by the money that was in the envelopes and that their hands were tied when it came to their finances. But I saw that they were never stressed or didn't fight about money. It made me wonder if the envelopes had anything to do with their healthy relationship."

"I began to feel a mix of emotions. I was envious of their financial stability, but at the same time, I felt scared that if I implemented a system like that in my business, I'd run out of money."

As is true for a lot of us investors, Jamie is constantly on the hunt to learn. She listened to podcasts and read books all the time. She had mentors in her life that gave her advice. After observing her friends on the envelope system, she knew she needed to educate herself on the financial side of her business. She started hearing people talk about *Profit First* on podcasts she listened to and mentors told her about the book, so she read it.

"After I read *Profit First,* the very first step told me to open bank accounts to manage my money," Jamie told me. "Fear still gripped me because I didn't want to feel chained in what I could spend. Thankfully, right after I read the book, I attended a mastermind and one of the people I respect the most in that group gave a presentation entirely on how implementing the bank accounts changed his business and life. That was the nudge I needed to start the system."

She added, "Opening those bank accounts completely changed my business and life. I realized one of my biggest enemies was fear. No one in my life taught me to manage finances of the business, so that lack of knowledge created anxiety. I know managing money is important, but I had to seek the knowledge for myself."

After reading *Profit First* and understanding the need to overcome her fear to live stress-free like her friends, Jamie knew she needed to take her first step and open up the bank accounts.

WHICH ACCOUNTS DO I SET UP AND WHAT ARE THEIR PURPOSES?

It's time to open bank accounts to separate your money into different "buckets" so that you can get a clear picture of your business and your cash position. One of the most common pushbacks I hear from real estate investors about the system is they may already have a few bank accounts, so setting up even more seems like too much work. You will use these new accounts to direct and manage your money, not just as a placeholder for a property or escrow account, even though you may have some of those as part of the system.

You are reading this book for a purpose. Don't let the first action step stop you. We are real estate investors, so we are already versed in the art of tackling objectives and conquering mountains. This is why I know you can make this first step work and ultimately make the whole system work for you.

Jamie's eyes opened when she saw her friends using the envelope system and how it gave them clarity in their finances. When she opened up the bank accounts for her business, instead of looking at all of her money in one bank account, she could see where she had allocated her money.

If you just have that one big "melting pot" account where every dollar from every single avenue of your business is stirred together, this system will save your sanity. You will now manage your money instead of it managing you.

Let's get to what you care about: which accounts to set up.

THE HOLDING ACCOUNT

Account #1: Income

This is essentially just a holding bucket for your income. After setting up this one, make sure to tell your title company or attorney, whomever handles your property closings and gets you your moolah, that you have a new account you want money transferred into. If you receive checks from tenants, title companies, or attorneys, deposit the money here. The money will then sit there until you transfer it out to the other accounts. This is why it's important to have your income separated from your operating expenses. At the beginning, some investors we worked with thought that it would be okay to combine the income and operating expenses to save on an extra account, but they quickly realized this threw a monkey wrench in their system. They'd forget sometimes if they had done their transfers because money went in and out from that one account all the time. I highly recommend setting up a separate **Income** account just to hold the money as it comes in from your property sales or your rental income.

THE GOLDEN TRIO ACCOUNTS

If you're a living breathing human being, you've probably heard of *Star Wars* or *Harry Potter*. If you've never heard of *Star Wars* or *Harry Potter*, I'd like to meet you because that means you've somehow managed to dodge all forms of media and marketing and that would make for a very interesting conversation. In both of those sagas there are three main heroes. In *Star Wars*, you have Luke, Han, and Leia (and that's just the original trilogy, which is all I will reference so as not to ignite a war). In *Harry Potter*, you have Harry, Ron, and Hermione. Many epic stories have three main heroes. These characters always push the story forward and the story revolves around these characters at all times.

Why do I go into this other than because I'm a total and complete nerd? Because your company needs three main heroes always working for you, battling against the cash-eating monster that the business has become. You need three accounts focused on saving your bacon and helping you vanquish the Emperor or He-Who-Must-Not-Be-Named (your enemies, for the jocks and cheerleaders reading this book) of your business that will constantly try to bleed your cash from your company. What are these three accounts? They are the **Profit, Owner's Comp**, and **Owner's Tax** accounts.

Account #2: The Profit Account

This account is to give you a return for running a successful company. Putting your first dollars here is how you stop losing out on the money you already made.

Isn't it fun to think about an account that is solely dedicated to the health and profitability of your company? You may say that you have a ton of bad debt that you need to get rid of first, and I really do understand a lot of real estate investors are in this position, but you still need a **Profit** account in your business into which you can transfer a percentage of cash every time money comes in. You need to live off less or pay your operating expenses with less money than 100% (or over 100%... yikes) of your income. You need a portion of that income to be for the health and profitability of your company. We will dive into how to pay down and crush debt in a later chapter, but for now, please set up a **Profit** account no matter where you stand in your business.

Account #3: The Owner's Comp Account

The **Profit** account is more for what your return on investment is for starting the business whereas the **Owner's Comp** account is more about compensating yourself for the work you do in the business. This is an account that ensures *you*, the owner, get paid. Say what? You mean you can actually run a business and get paid too? So many real estate investors do not pay themselves. You might be in this position right now, and just so you know, you are not alone by a longshot. But we need to do something about it. If you perform any part of the operations of the business, you should pay yourself a salary.

Disclaimer, I am not a CPA or tax professional, just a school of hard knocks graduate. If you put in the work, whether it be taking calls, going on appointments, running the marketing, managing the rehab, selling the properties, running property management, collecting rent, or really any part of the actual jobs of your company, you need to be compensated. You also need to think about what kind of salary or pay it would take to replace the seats you sit in right now. That doesn't mean if you do everything that you take the full amount of what you *should* be paid out of your business right from the start. It means realistically, if you can't afford to pay yourself anything, how will you be able to pay someone to replace you?

This is why many real estate investors scale their businesses unprofitably, because they don't know if they make enough to hire a replacement for the seats they sit in, but still hire people anyway and pray that they close enough deals to cover all the expenses. Having an account dedicated to paying yourself can help you see if you can pay yourself what you need and then see if you have enough to replace yourself in some of the jobs you hold in your company.

Let me vent a little here on your behalf. You started the dang business. You put in blood, sweat, tears, and years of toil. You got up early and stayed up late to take seller calls or go to job sites or read BiggerPockets blogs on how to fix an issue that just came up. You are your best employee, bar none. No one will *ever* care for your business like you do. You may have others who work in your business that give their all and are the best team members possible, but you will always care about your business the most. You need to pay yourself something. You can't keep feeding the monster without a return on that investment. Set up an **Owner's Comp** account and start allocating money to pay yourself!

Account #4: Owner's Tax Account

This account will blow your mind. You can save for taxes throughout the year instead of scrambling at tax time to close just one more deal to pay your taxes! Gasp! This account is for *you,* the owner, to pay your taxes. This is not a property tax account, which we will talk about later, and this is not a tax account to pay your employees' payroll tax. This account is for *you.* The business should save to pay your taxes because you pay taxes on the income generated from your business.

Do you see why I call these the Golden Trio? Because they really are the heroes of your business that you've never had before. These accounts are to make sure *you* and your business are healthy and that *you* have control over your finances. You've worked too hard and long to not have your business work for you. Become the hero of your business and financial journey and set these accounts up to force yourself to take your profit first and become profitable. If you can fund these accounts to where they should be and are able to support the business on the rest of the revenue, you know that you have an actual business that pays you and is able to take care of its responsibilities. Just think of how you will feel when that happens.

THE OPERATING EXPENSE ACCOUNT

Account #5: The Operating Expense Account

You may not have to open a new account for your operating expenses. I'd recommend using the account that already handles your operating expenses. Instead of all your money funneling into this big pot, now you have other accounts to save for taxes, pay yourself, and hold your profit. Now you'll see what it truly takes to run your business.

THE ACCOUNT THAT COULD SAVE YOUR BUSINESS FROM A PONZI SCHEME

Account #6: The OPM Account

The **OPM (Other People's Money)** account is specifically for when you get money from a hard money or private money lender to fix up a property and then sell it. Any short-term loans should go into this account. That way, you separate your money (the first five accounts) from what is **Other People's Money**. Can you see how powerful this is? When you separate other people's money from yours, you will know what kind of cash it takes to run your business. The money in this **OPM** account is to be spent only on properties for which those funds have been designated for rehab. If you have to dip into this account to run the operations of your business, it's a huge red warning light to you that your business doesn't have enough income coming in to keep your company running without relying on the money you borrowed for specific projects.

Please stop using your private lenders' funds for anything but the project it was designated for. If you go over budget on the rehab (which never happens, right?), you have a couple of options. If you have more equity to borrow against, you can reach out to the lender for additional funds, or you will have to dip into your own resources.

If you have a lot of flips going on at the same time, you may want to consider opening up a new account per lender to know how much a specific lender has given and keep the money even more separate, but that's totally up to you. I'll go over this more in-depth in the "Advanced Accounts" section of chapter nine.

IF YOU'RE A BUY AND HOLD INVESTOR, WHICH ACCOUNTS APPLY TO YOU?

If you hold rental properties and aren't just fixing and flipping or wholesaling, you still need the same foundational accounts. You still need to take your profit first and pay yourself. You might not need to save as much in the **Owner's Tax** account because of how much you can depreciate and save on your personal taxes with your rentals, but you should still have the **Owner's Tax** account. What other accounts should you have if you hold properties long-term?

Buy and Hold Account 1: PITI

PITI stands for Principal, Interest, (Property) Taxes, and Insurance. One of your biggest expenses will more than likely be the mortgages you have on your rentals unless you own them free and clear. An account just for PITI has been game-changing for the buy and hold investors we work with because they now can see at a glance what they will pay every month for their mortgages. This also helps save for property taxes and insurance that you may pay monthly, biannually, annually, and so on. Instead of having to try and scrounge up money at the end of the year to pay a big property tax bill, you will save for that property tax bill throughout the year and give yourself a lot of breathing room.

Buy and Hold Account 2:
Rental Repairs/Maintenance, Vacancy, and Turnover

The biggest expenses you'll have as a buy and hold investor will be repairs, vacancy, and turnover. When you bought your rentals, you probably estimated a percentage for repairs, vacancy, and turnover to factor what your cash flow would be. Because you already took that into consideration up front, you can set up an account to transfer the estimated percentage every month to see if the amount that you set when purchasing your rentals was realistic. This also makes sure you have the money for repairs, vacancy, and turnover *when* it happens.

BONUS TIP

You *need* to set up an account for the tenants' security deposits. Please do not mix security deposits with any other money.

TWO MORE ACCOUNTS TO CONSIDER USING

Bonus Account: Bad Debt

To get started, a lot of investors finance a lot of purchases with credit cards or with unsecured loans and may keep in that habit as the business grows. Having an account to pay down this debt brings peace of mind and helps you focus on eliminating the bad debt in your business.

Bonus Account: Giving/Charity

I encourage you to consider opening an account for the sole purpose of charitable contributions. The investors who give are the ones who are the most successful and the happiest internally. My company has an account dedicated to charity because giving is one of my core values. We support several missions' teams and the blessings to our company are evident. Several investors we work with have this account, and they are the clients who have a lot less stress and have great peace.

DO I REALLY NEED ALL OF THESE ACCOUNTS?

You may be thinking, *Why all of these accounts?* You can see that each one has a very specific purpose. PFREI is *not* about setting up bank accounts. Setting up the accounts is a step in the process. The purpose of the system is to help you make more money without having to do more deals. It's to unlock your why and put you back in control of your business. The accounts are a step in the journey toward achieving those goals.

A lot of investors have even more than this to separate their money. I dive into these later in the book to show you how to supercharge your business with different accounts.

If you have a lot of entities, you may also think, *Do I need to set up all of these accounts for each entity?* I'll go more in depth on this in chapter eight, but overall the answer is if the different entities are completely different businesses (think fix-and-flipping versus just holding rentals) then yes, you should set up the accounts for the different businesses. If you have several limited liability companies (LLCs) that just hold rentals or are similar businesses, you can use the same accounts for different entities to see the health of all your rentals. In the end, you want this system to work with you and for you. The end goal is to manage your money and not have it manage you. Do not be afraid to tweak the system to what *you* need in your business.

BANK BALANCE MONEY MANAGEMENT

After implementing Profit First in real estate investing businesses and in my own businesses, I've learned that when the accounts are set up, they bring incredible clarity and confidence. In my own business, the bank accounts let me know when I can hire a new employee and when I have to wait. When I have at least three months reserves in the **Operating Expense** account to cover a new employee, I know I can hire someone. This is how you scale profitably. A lot of investors and business owners hire when they need someone and don't take the true cost into account at all. If you have the bank accounts set up, you can quickly see whether you can take someone on by the amount you have in your account.

The fact that you can leverage checking your bank accounts and their balances on a daily basis to your advantage is so powerful. You more than likely log into your bank daily and look at your bank account (singular). If there is a lot of money, you feel pretty good. If there isn't a lot of money, you go into panic mode. Not only do you go into panic mode, but you also have *no* idea where and how the money in the account got that low. Separating that one account into the foundational accounts will allow you to see right away if you have enough to pay yourself, what kind of profit your company makes, how much you have to pay the expenses of the business, and how much you have left to spend on your rehabs in the **OPM** account. Do you now see how you'll be able to look at your bank accounts and know the health of your business at a glance without having to dive into your financial statements on a daily basis? If this doesn't get you excited about finally having control over your profit and finances, I don't know what will.

Separating the profit from your deals and rentals will help right away be able to make and keep more money without doing any more deals. You will be a savvier business owner just by taking this first step. We really are creatures of habit. Leverage the habit of looking at your bank accounts to your advantage to help you have a greater understanding of where your business stands.

WHICH BANK SHOULD I CHOOSE TO SET UP MY ACCOUNTS?

This is a question people ask me all the time. The bottom line is you are looking for a bank with:

- No fee accounts
- Easy access to main checking accounts
- A banker who likes the Profit First model

Go to simplecfosolutions.com/pfrei for a list of recommended banks for setting up the accounts.

SEEING THE LIGHT

Jamie told me, "After setting up the accounts and learning my TAPs and CAPs, I knew my finances had to change. I dove into my expenses, and I had some drastic cuts to make. I cut all of my operating expenses by 50% over the first few months I ran Profit First because I was determined to get my business in shape. This included letting go of two people on my team because I had to make sure that every seat brought in revenue. This was the hardest decision I had to make."

"Before Profit First I took some of my pay and the profit from the business and 'reinvested' it to make sure I could keep paying people instead of analyzing whether every person did what needed to be done," Jamie continued. "Once I ran on Profit First, I had the knowledge to know whether a seat performed profitably. After cutting expenses and letting people go, I started to see growth. It shocked me how much we grew by making those changes."

A lot of investors might think that by cutting expenses and letting people go you are going backwards, when in reality, if you make those decisions based on information and knowledge of your business, those steps help push your company forward.

Jamie saw results in her business right away. After about two months of running on Profit First, her accounts started filling up. She told me, "That made me feel so much more secure than the system or lack of a system I had before when it came to my finances. Seeing the different accounts grow gave me a tremendous amount of stress relief and made me feel like I didn't need to be on the constant chase for the next deal. I had finally stopped living deal to deal!"

The Profit First system changed Jamie's business and personal life on a deep level. "The quality of my life was drastically different after implementing Profit First. Today I am more profitable than I ever have been. I don't worry about my finances anymore. Now that I have a simple system for my finances, I have been able to put people in place to run the business and manage the finances through the Profit First system and that has given me my life back. I am able to work about one hour a day in the investing business and now I spend my time working on the mastermind I help run. I also help coach my daughter's volleyball games. Without Profit First, I wouldn't have felt comfortable being away from the business, but this system has given me so much security and helped me focus on what I want to."

Jamie knows the power of this system, and I hope seeing her story prompts you take action so you can start your own journey.

START NOW

If you aren't excited to open more accounts right this second, then I have failed in the explanation of how this system will help you put more money in your pocket—immediately. I have talked to hundreds of investors who wish they would have started this system years earlier. These are people with multiple entities and businesses doing millions of dollars a year in property profit and sales. If you want to emulate them and get started on the path right now, here is what you need to do:

1. Pick a bank to set up the accounts. You can go to simplecfosolutions.com/pfrei for the list of Profit First friendly banks. Start calling the banks right now to set an appointment.

2. Set up the PFREI foundational accounts: **Income, Profit, Owner's Comp, Owner's Tax, OpEx,** and **OPM.**

Taking these actions is a *huge* step on your journey to putting and keeping more money in your pocket with the same number of deals you're doing now. Living deal to deal will be a thing of the past as you implement the action steps of this chapter and the following chapters.

Chapter 5

STEP THREE: THE REAL ESTATE RHYTHM

"My companies are like lost children that have come home."

This is an exact quote from D.J. Savoy. He said this to me after we implemented PFREI in his selling companies.

D.J. came to us with his books a mess and in need of some clarification. For the different companies he owns, he has seven entities. We started PFREI for his two selling companies. First we asked D.J. to open his foundational bank accounts for both selling entities. Then, we took the Real Revenue from the properties he sold and identified the percentages he could allocate and transfer to his different accounts.

Because he still needed help to get his books to 100% complete and clean, we started with higher percentages for his **Operating Expense** account and lower percentages for his "golden trio," the **Profit, Owner's Comp,** and **Owner's Tax** accounts. D.J. had a goal to save three months' worth of operating expenses because he wanted the peace of mind those reserves would provide. We also began allocating more funds to save for his goal.

We then created a rhythm: We met every other Friday to run the allocations.

I'm glad D.J. made it a mission to save extra for his expenses because, several months into our work together, two hurricanes came through his area. They created a lot of chaos. Many of his rental units were damaged, his employees were displaced from their homes for months, and he ran around like a chicken with his head cut off in order to keep his companies functioning.

One of the best meetings we had was about a month after the hurricanes. Even through all the mayhem, D.J. still managed to sell a couple deals because he and his team are rock stars (shout-out to Morgyn Grady on D.J.'s team). Because his numbers were clear, we were able to go over the balances in his accounts from previous allocations and project how many months of operating expenses he had. He had achieved his savings goal, and because he had several months' worth of expenses, he could take a little breather from all the chaos of the hurricanes.

I'll never forget one allocation meeting we had with D.J.. When it was over he said, "Before PFREI, it was like we played a game but had no idea which game it was or any idea how to keep score. We were always on the defensive, but with no end in sight. Now after running this system, we not only know which game we are playing, but we are in control of the game, know where we are at all times, and are able to go on the offensive and build and grow the business. PFREI and the allocations have been a total game changer."

Setting up the accounts and allocating (transferring) the money based on your TAPs gives you the clarity you need to reach any financial goal you have for your business. This rhythm helps you stay on track. I like to call this the Real Estate Rhythm because it is unique to real estate investing. This rhythm helps maintain your sanity in the worst of times when you have to focus on everything *but* the finances. No matter the circumstances, whether it be hurricanes or windfalls of money, if you have a rhythm to transfer your Real Revenue into the bank accounts you set up, you will harness the power of PFREI in *your* business.

WHAT ARE ALLOCATIONS?

Before we move on, let's make sure you are clear on allocations—the funds transfers you will make into your different accounts based on the percentages you've assigned for your business. Do you remember the short section about CAPs or Current Allocation Percentages? These numbers are based on what you currently spend. You can get your bookkeeper to help you come up with your CAPs or look at your profit and loss statement to figure out how much you've been spending in a month. Then, take that number and divide it by your typical monthly Real Revenue number to get the percent you've been spending on the operations of your business. For example, let's say you have $20,000 in expenses and $30,000 in Real Revenue. When you divide the expenses by the Real Revenue you get 67%. This would be the percentage you spend on operational expenses.

I've seen this number be very high for investors, so don't completely freak out. A great benefit of Profit First is to show you how high your expenses are and to fight to either get them down or to drive your Real Revenue up.

If you don't have clean books yet or can't get this percentage from your bookkeeper, do *not* let this stop you. Start with 97% for your operating expenses and 1% to each of your "golden trio" accounts. The point is to start taking your profit first in order to get a different result financially than you ever have before. This helps you stop living that deal-to-deal cycle, so please don't let anything stop you from beginning the allocations.

SAMPE PERCENTAGES	
Account Name	CAPs
Profit	5%
Owner's Comp	10%
Owner's Tax	15%
Operating Expenses	70%

After you have your estimated expense percentage, you can start filling in the rest of your CAPs. Above is a sample of what we do with investors and how we show the percentages.

The CAPs column is the percentage you can currently commit to transferring every time you run the allocations. Here are the formulas again for Real Revenue:

Formula for finding Real Revenue for a Selling Company: Sales Price *minus* Pass Through Revenue (purchase price *plus* rehab costs *plus* closing costs *plus* holding costs *plus* interest paid to lender) *equals* Real Revenue

Formula for finding Real Revenue for a Rental Company: Rental Income *plus* Owner Finance Income *minus* Pass Through Revenue (PITI) *equals* Real Revenue

Now that you have the Real Revenue number, your CAPs are the percentages you've chosen to transfer into those specific accounts. The Sample Allocations table is an example.

SAMPLE ALLOCATIONS		
Account Name	CAPs	Amounts
Real Revenue		$20,000
Profit	5%	$1,000
Owner's Comp	10%	$2,000
Owner's Tax	15%	$3,000
Operating Expenses	70%	$14,000

I want to make this as easy as possible for you, so if you go to simplecfosolutions.com/pfrei, you can grab the Allocation Calculator we use with real estate investors to make running the allocations easy as pie.

WHAT TO DO IF YOUR EXPENSE PERCENTAGE IS TOO HIGH

As you begin allocating your percentages, your operating expenses might turn out to be higher than you expected. When you see this, you might have a slight panic attack. If you were being honest, facing your expenses is one reason you probably hesitated to pick up this book: You didn't want to have to accept the monster that is your finances. Now, you're facing it, so if you feel panicked, just remind yourself that there is a process to analyze and cut expenses.

I love the framework for how to slash expenses Mike Michalowicz gives in *Profit First*. It takes dedication, but if you want to get out of the deal-to-deal cycle and want to get your business healthy, you need to put in the work.

Here are the steps to gain clarity on the expenses and know which ones to cut:

1. Print out your bank and credit card statements for the last month.

2. Next to each expense item on the statements, categorize them by three letters: P, R, and U.
    a. P is for Profitable. This expense drives revenue, brings profit to your company, or saves you a ton of time and headache. Write the letter *P* next to these expenses.
    b. R is for Replaceable. This expense can be replaced by something cheaper or by an option that will have a greater return. Write the letter *R* next to these expenses.
    c. U is for Unnecessary. These expenses will be items such as the subscriptions that you have that you never use or expenses that don't drive revenue, bring profit to your company, or save you a ton of time and headaches. Write the letter *U* next to these expenses and circle them with a red pen.

3. After you've put the letters next to each expense and circled the Unnecessary expenses, meet with your team to start cutting the Unnecessary expenses and decide what Replaceable expenses you can switch out right away with a more efficient expense.

4. Print out a list of all your team members and write down the same letters next to each name (P, R, or U).

a. This will most likely be the most painful part of the whole exercise, but you need to make sure each and every team member pulls their weight and either brings in revenue (like great sales people), protects the revenue (like great finance people), or saves you time (like operations and administrative people) to focus on higher level tasks.

b. Anyone with a U next to their name needs a plan for going out the door as soon as possible.

c. If you placed an R next to a team member's name, you know in your heart you more than likely need to replace them. If you want to see if they can rise to your standard, give them a goal and time frame to become profitable, but if they don't hit it, you need to replace them. If they can be replaced by a system or automation, put that system in place. If that team member is still a fit for the company and you have a seat for them, put them in another seat.

d. For the team members you've written a P next to, who drive profitability or save you time and headaches to work on bigger tasks, tell them they're appreciated. Write a handwritten note, take them to lunch, give them a gift. These are the people that help you build your business and need to know you care.

I know this exercise will be uncomfortable, but hasn't worrying every day about your finances been uncomfortable up to this point? This will help you see where you stand when it comes to your expenses, including payments to team members, and determine what you need in order to run your business in the best way possible.

You have a responsibility to yourself, your business, your team members, your family, and anyone else who relies on you to get your expenses under control. The number one reason you'll go out of business is letting your costs run wild. Don't let yourself and your team down by not doing what needs to be done.

The other side of the coin is to increase the revenue. All of the money spent really should drive or protect things, or help you save time and stress. If you already run a lean operation, you may have a revenue problem and need to drive more deals into your business. This isn't a book on marketing, but you can use PFREI to help you figure out the best ways for you to market, which I cover in Chapter 9.

WHEN TO RUN ALLOCATIONS

Profit First for Real Estate Investing is a *system* for managing your finances. Systems are built on processes and automation, so you need to get into a rhythm of managing the finances and running the allocations. Your business is different than a typical "brick and mortar" business, so you need to create your own rhythm based on when it's best for *you* to run the allocations.

Let's get to what you care about: Depending on the size of your business and the number of properties you are selling, you will have several options for running allocations.

1. Selling a property once a week.
   If you are selling at least one property a week, I'd run the allocations and transfer the money on a weekly basis. Pick a day of the week and consistently transfer the

money into the accounts based on your percentages on that day.

2. Selling one to two properties a month.
   In this case, you can use the method of transferring on certain days of the month, such as the 1st and 15th or the 10th and 25th.

3. Selling a couple properties every quarter.
   Run the allocation every time you sell a property and not on a certain day or date. You might think, *Doesn't that defeat the purpose of a rhythm?* The rhythm comes from knowing you're allocating the Real Revenue for several months at a time. This is how you even out your cash flow when you're not selling as many properties.

   We have a client who sells one or two properties a quarter. We run the allocations with him when he sells the properties, and he makes sure to cover what he needs in **Profit**, **Owner's Comp**, **Owner's Tax**, and **Operating Expense** for several months at a time. It helps even out his cash flow even though he doesn't sell one every week or month.

4. Rental income allocations.
   For rentals, I have found that running allocations for the previous month around the 5th of the month is the best way to transfer the money. Most of the money collected is a mixture of rent that is due currently, rent collected early, and past due rent that is late. To create a standard for the allocations, look at the physical cash you brought in from the first day to the last day of the previous month, subtract the PITI from the physical

cash brought in to get the Real Revenue, and now you have what you can allocate to the different accounts you have set up for your rental business.

For example, say in September you collected $10,000 in cash, which was a mixture of past due, current, early rent payments, and late fees. Your PITI was $6,000 for September, so the Real Revenue left over would be $4,000 to allocate around October 5 for September.

Visually it looks like this:

$10,000   (TOTAL COLLECTIONS IN SEPTEMBER)
-   $6,000   (PITI)
= $4,000   (REAL REVENUE)

After you've figured out which allocation rhythm best fits your current situation, the next step is to transfer the money. Before we get into that, a disclaimer: If you say that none of these options fit your situation, then you need to figure out a rhythm that works for *you*. The whole point is to get into the *habit* of transferring your Real Revenue into the different accounts. Do what works for *you* and *your company,* an approach you can maintain consistently.

At this point, transferring the money is really simple. If you've run the allocations, you know the amounts that you can transfer into the respective accounts based on your CAPs. I recommend running the first several transfers yourself even if you have a team. This helps you see the money filling the accounts and how the system works. From there you can have your team members transfer the money on your allocation day if you have someone in the finance seat.

This is it. This is how you manage your money as a real estate investor. I know it sounds so simple, and in reality, it is. It takes discipline and determination to run the allocations and make the transfers, but the system was created to be as simple as humanly possible and to work with what you do already.

You may run into objections from your bookkeeper, who is concerned that this approach will add too much to their duties. That's a load of bull. Setting up the accounts in the finance software, such as QuickBooks Online, will take one tenth of the time of setting up the physical bank accounts. Transferring the money to the different accounts takes about an extra five seconds to input a transfer from one account to another. Do *not* let anyone use this excuse to not run the PFREI system.

YOU WILL RUN INTO THIS SITUATION

There is a situation you *will* encounter when you run the allocations as a real estate investor. When you run a Profit and Loss statement (P&L) on a property that you just sold, the profit you make on the property more than likely will be different than the actual cash you receive in your bank account. The exception is when you do an assignment of contract and literally get the assignment fee and have no costs associated with the property contract you assigned.

Why is your profit different than the actual cash received? The most likely scenario is you put your own money into the property during the rehab because you went over budget and the loan you received for the project didn't cover all the expenses for the property. That money you put in yourself will be returned above and beyond the profit received at the closing table.

Real Revenue or the Property Profit is *not* affected by the loan amount. The Real Revenue factors in the sales price *minus* all the costs associated with the property. This is an internal number to show you what you made per deal, and you'll get the Real Revenue from your bookkeeper after they run a P&L on that house when it closes.

The cash received at closing *is* affected by the loan amount because the title company or attorney that performs the closing doesn't care about what you spent on the property. They care about the sales price, paying back the loan to the lender, and making sure the closing costs are covered.

To simplify, say you as the investor bought a property for $50,000. You got a loan for $65,000 because you thought the rehab would cost $15,000 and then you sold it for $100,000. In reality, you spent $20,000 on the rehab because it cost more than you planned. Let's break down the difference between calculating the Real Revenue for the property, the cash received at closing, and the difference between them.

Real Revenue calculation:

	$100,000	(SALES PRICE)
−	$50,000	(PURCHASE PRICE)
−	$20,000	(OVER BUDGET RENOVATION COSTS)
−	$10,000	(HOLDING AND CLOSING COSTS)
=	$20,000	(REAL REVENUE)

Cash Received from Closing calculation:

	$100,000	(SALES PRICE)
−	$65,000	(LOAN AMOUNT THAT INCLUDES PURCHASE PRICE *PLUS* BUDGETED RENOVATION COSTS)
−	$10,000	(HOLDING AND CLOSING COSTS)
=	$25,000	(CASH RECEIVED AT CLOSING)

In this example, you received $25,000 but the Real Revenue was $20,000. That extra $5,000 you received was the money you put in yourself to cover the extra cost. That $5,000 needs to first be transferred to whichever account it came from and then the $20,000 in Real Revenue will follow the standard allocation process.

Going over budget and spending your own money on rehabs happens *all* the time. Do you see that if you fix-and- flip a lot of properties a year and are always underfunded, your own money spent on those deals can add up very quickly? What's more, your money doesn't get refunded back to you until the closing happens. You could end up with $5,000, $10,000, $50,000, or $100,000 of your own money into your properties if you aren't careful, and then you wonder where all your "profit" is. See why knowing your numbers is so important?

If you come in under budget on a project and do *not* use all of the lender's funds to renovate the property, when the property closes, the extra funds from the lender still sitting in your bank account are now a part of your profit. The lender is paid off on the HUD at the closing table, so any extra funds from their loan in your **OPM** account are now part of the profit of the property and can be transferred to the **Income** account to be allocated with the rest of the funds from the closing. Here's another with the same numbers except the renovation costs are now under budget.

Real Revenue calculation:

	$100,000	(SALES PRICE)
−	$50,000	(PURCHASE PRICE)
−	$10,000	(UNDER BUDGET RENOVATION COST)
−	$10,000	(HOLDING AND CLOSING COSTS)
=	$30,000	(REAL REVENUE)

Cash Received from Closing calculation:

	$100,000	(SALES PRICE)
−	$65,000	(LOAN AMOUNT THAT INCLUDES PURCHASE PRICE *PLUS* BUDGETED RENOVATION COSTS)
−	$10,000	(HOLDING AND CLOSING COSTS)
=	$25,000	(CASH RECEIVED AT CLOSING)

Cash in OPM to transfer to Income:

	$65,000	(LOAN AMOUNT RECEIVED)
−	$50,000	(PURCHASE PRICE)
−	$10,000	(RENOVATION COSTS)
=	$5,000	(MONEY LEFT OVER IN **OPM** ACCOUNT NOT SPENT ON REHAB BECAUSE YOU CAME UNDER BUDGET)

You can now transfer that $5,000 to the **Income** account because you can see your Real Revenue is $30,000, but you only received $25,000 at closing because that other $5,000 is still in your **OPM** account from unspent renovation funds because you were under budget.

READ THIS IF YOU *STILL* DON'T WANT TO RUN ALLOCATIONS AND TRANSFER MONEY

The true power in the Profit First for Real Estate Investing system is to make your financial management run like clockwork. When I first ran the allocations and transferred the money in my business, it took all the guesswork out of my finances and helped me determine if I brought enough in to support the team, the company, and myself. It is truly eye-opening when you begin the allocations.

I've been very fortunate to work with some amazing real estate investors. One of those investors is Rich Lennon. In Chapter 7, I tell you the story of how we got his books cleaned up and how life-changing that was, but in this section I want to tell you how the PFREI system transformed Rich's business.

Rich was like most investors in that he had multiple bank accounts, but he didn't use them to keep track of his business. He operated from one main bank account for all of his business and made decisions based on how much money was in the account. He felt great when there was a lot of money in there and stressed when the balance was low.

Up to this point, Rich had really never paid himself from his businesses and wanted to sell more properties and grow his rental portfolio. When we implemented PFREI and designated bank accounts for specific areas of his business such as **Profit**, **Owner's Comp**, **Owner's Taxes**, and **Operating Expenses**, he gained even more clarity, and it forced him to think about paying himself.

Another benefit separating his funds from that one bank account was that he could see how much he had in his business for his benefit versus what he had to spend on expenses. Having this clarity helped him make some major decisions when the pandemic of 2020 hit. With no clear path of how this global event would play out, he was able to see how much in his business he had to live on for months at a time if all of his income from his rentals or flips dried up. He did some major restructuring in his business long before it was too late.

PFREI and the allocations gave Rich more clarity in his business and helped him make decisions long before there was a major problem in his business. Today he is able to switch to whatever model he wants to (for example, wholesaling, rentals, flips, and so on) based on which option would be the biggest return for him at the moment. This is the power and clarity that PFREI gives to you and your business.

QUARTERLY PROFIT DISTRIBUTIONS

This system will change your life in the day-to-day and at a high level. You'll also see the money start piling up in the different accounts, and one of those accounts is the **Profit** account. Every quarter, it will be obvious if your company has done well or not by the amount of money you have been able to deposit and keep in this account. This money is for you as the owner as a return on investment for the risk you took to start the business and have it run like a well-oiled machine.

Every quarter, take up to 50% out of the account and distribute it to yourself to do whatever you want to with that money. Do *not* rely on this money to pay yourself or to bank on as part of your salary. This should be a reward above and beyond what you pay yourself. Then use the money in any way you want to. Give to others, go on a vacation with your family, buy that car you've always wanted to. The point is to give yourself a reason to be happy that you started the business, and that the business returns all that you've poured into it.

AUTOMATE EVERYTHING YOU CAN

While we're on the subject of getting into a rhythm with your finances, how about the other side of the coin? We've talked about what to do when money comes in and to transfer it to the appropriate accounts, but what about when money needs to come out of the accounts for bills and running the business?

I suggest automating every part of your business that you possibly can, and that includes making payments. With the

Profit First system in place, you will have a much better grasp on where your money goes, so set up as many auto payments to vendors and websites as you can.

If you still cut a lot of paper checks every week or every month, please know there are better, faster, and more efficient ways to get the bills paid. There are systems inside your accounting software as well as specific sites like Bill.com that can automate a lot of your financial processes to take even more routine tasks off you and your team's plate.

START NOW

This call to action is one of the most important because after you get in the rhythm of transfers, you help your business even out the cash flow and take control over your finances. When you start implementing the action steps of this chapter and stick with them long-term, you can finally stop living the deal-to-deal cycle and free yourself from constant stress.

1. Figure out your current expense percentage. Get your financial statements and find the average of what you currently spend on your expenses and divide that number by your average Real Revenue (use at least a six month time frame).

2. Run the P, R, and U exercise on your business's expenses and on your team members to make sure every dollar going out the door is driving or protecting revenue, or helping you save time and stress.

3. Plan your CAPs, what you need for the **Profit**, **Owner's Comp**, **Owner's Tax**, and **Operating Expense** accounts. Use these percentages when you run allocations.

4. The next time a property sells, or at the end of month for rentals, get your first allocation ready by finding the Real Revenue and plugging in your percentages. If you want a template to plug your numbers into to make it as simple as possible, go to simplecfosolutions.com/pfrei.

5. After you have the Real Revenue dollar amounts to allocate, transfer the money from the **Income** account to the respective accounts.

6. Every quarter, remember to take some sort of draw from the **Profit** account to celebrate the new health of your company and to reward yourself for managing the finances and running a true business.

Chapter 6

WHY NOT SPENDING EVERY DIME WILL HELP YOU SCALE PROFITABLY

It started like any other Sunday. I got up, spent quiet time in the morning by myself, and then got ready for church. My wife, Angela, looked as beautiful as always as we drove to church together. We settled into our seats as the guest speaker began teaching.

Then I felt it. An impending sense of doom. My heart started beating faster, and I sensed something was wrong. My vision started swimming, and I had trouble breathing. I told my wife, "I don't feel good and need to go to the bathroom."

Angela escorted me out of the room to the nearest restroom as I struggled to breathe. I had no idea what was going on, but I knew I needed help.

I am the stereotypical man who does not go to the doctor for most reasons. I hate spending a ton of money, especially on doctor visits, but I knew this time something was different, and I should see someone.

I felt as though my heart was beating outside of my chest. "I need to go the emergency room," I told Angela. "I think I might be having a heart attack."

She rushed me to the closest hospital, and I told the nurses my symptoms. They escorted me to the back rooms right away as other people stood in line because the ER treats heart problems immediately. The nurses hooked me up to the EKG machines and ran a bunch of tests on me. They were able to tell right away that I didn't have a heart attack.

The doctor eventually came back to my room and told me that all tests came back okay and that it may have been an anxiety attack. Turns out a crazy work schedule, my wife being pregnant with our first child, and investing in real estate on the side can be a little nerve-racking! Who knew?! As I lay in the hospital bed, I was thankful it wasn't a heart attack. I sat thinking I was very glad I had reserves in my bank account to cover emergencies just like this. Money was "one less thing" to worry about because I had a lot of other stress, apparently.

You are a human being. You are also a real estate investor. You are going to have stress in your life. Money should be one less thing to worry about, just like our buddy Forrest Gump tells us. As you begin to allocate money into different accounts, you will start to accumulate reserves. If you are like most investors, you haven't held on to any money you've made for very long. You won't know what to do with the extra cash or what it's purpose is, so let me guide you to give you one less thing to worry about.

WHY WOULD I LET ALL OF THAT MONEY JUST SIT THERE?

We investors know that lazy money is almost a cardinal sin. We can't stand to see funds sit in an account. We want it to be out on the streets making us more. How dare any cash at all be left in our accounts! While I applaud wanting all your dollars working for you all the time, not everything sitting in accounts is "lazy." I want to challenge your thinking and tell you that the key to growth is through reserves, not spending every dollar you make.

In September of 2016, Chase Bank conducted research on how many cash buffer days the average small business has.[1] Cash buffer days are defined as the number of days a business could pay its expenses without any new sales or income being generated and received. The average number of cash buffer days was twenty-seven. In other words, the average business has less than one month held in reserves.

As a real estate investor, you may look at that and say, "I wish I had twenty-seven days of cash reserves in the bank! My money is always going in and out and I'm lucky if I have five days of cash reserves at one time." I don't want you to panic every day, week, and month because your cash flow is always so up and down.

After you start moving money into the **Profit** and **Owner's Tax** account, you'll begin to see money stockpiling. This is your fork in the road. Do you let the money sit there, providing you with the ability to pay your bills, taxes, and *yourself* on time? Or do you pull that money out of the accounts and use it to make *more* money by purchasing a deal, lending it out, or investing it into a multitude of different things?

At this fork in the road, let me ask you: What is the cost of not having the money in the account when you need it?

We, as investors, view money differently than the typical business owner because we know that we can make money with our money. Most small businesses who run a labor-intensive business, such as a restaurant, try to keep costs as low as

[1] https://www.jpmorganchase.com/institute/research/small-business/report-cash-flows-balances-and-buffer-days.htm#finding-3

possible all the time and don't think of the money they spend as investments. But we look at almost every dollar spent as an investment that gives a return on that money. I get why it might be hard to have accounts that are specifically set up to *not* spend.

So why would you let all that money sit there?

Let's get to what you care about: There are several reasons to build cash reserves.

1. Reserves are the way to profitable growth.

You may be wondering, *How can keeping cash in my accounts and not spending grow my business?* Let me explain. Lenders love to see cash in accounts. It shows them that you have the financial discipline to hang onto money for the rainy days of the business, and that you have the cash on hand to pivot if something goes south in your business. One of the clients we work with had a private lender ask how much they had in reserves in their business because he wouldn't lend unless they had a certain dollar amount.

Reserves are an investment in yourself and your business to be able to get more funding and more deals than if you used every dime for a new deal. Think about that. Leaving money in your accounts can end up making you more money than "reinvesting" every dollar because you can do way more deals using other people's money than constantly taking your reserves out for every property. If you want to scale your business the right way, you need your own reserves. You will want and need to use lender's funds to take yourself to the next level and do more deals.

If you always spend every dime, you run on fumes. You won't think of growing the business but of just going after that next house. If you *need* that next deal to be able to cover your expenses or taxes, you will end up buying properties you never should have. Reserves help to give your brain breathing room to make the best decisions without the pressure of *needing* that next property.

With reserves, you can also make the best decisions about hiring people. If you have extra money in the accounts, you can hire someone without worrying if you will be able to pay them. This is the way to grow profitably and hire like a business owner.

2. It offers security for your people.

I worked with one investor who struggled with this concept of keeping several months' worth of reserves in his account.

He asked me, "Why should I keep reserves in the accounts when I could invest them?"

Knowing he had people on payroll, I asked him, "What or who are the best investments in your business? If everyone who worked with you walked away from your business right now because you aren't able to pay them, how well would the business run?"

I could see the light bulb turn on over his head. "The reserves aren't just for me. I need to make sure my people have security and peace of mind. That money in the Profit, Tax, or Emergency accounts is there to make sure if something catastrophic happened to the business, we wouldn't go out of business overnight. Those reserves are my investment in my people and business."

Your employees need security from you. *Staying* in business means just as much to the people who work with you as it does to you. They want the company to be healthy. They want the confidence that you know how to manage the finances and how to build cash reserves. They want the security of the job you provide them.

If you go through a rough patch in the business and are able to get in front of it by making confident decisions based on your finances and data, you will inspire your team and they will do everything they can to help right the ship again. But if you don't know where you stand or have key indicators, you won't be able to unlock this huge business saving strategy in your company.

3. It provides peace of mind for yourself.

Don't forget about yourself. I know we, as real estate investors, are able to handle a lot more risk than most people, but the investors who build successful businesses have reserves. The fact that they have reserves—not the number of deals they do—is a mark of a successful business.

Money in the accounts will give you peace of mind. Just like when I was in the hospital and didn't have to think about the cost, you don't want to stress over the decisions you need to make for your business. If you ever get in a really bad jam, you'll have the confidence that you won't run out of cash and have to go belly up on the spot. Those reserves give security in the fact that you have the money to pay the IRS what they require. When you hold reserves you also prove to yourself that you are a business owner who knows how to handle his finances. That confidence comes through your own actions.

I wrote this book during the COVID-19 pandemic. No one in the real estate investing world—and I won't fall down the conspiracy theorist rabbit hole—saw the pandemic coming and how it would affect businesses. The state of Pennsylvania ruled that real estate was a "nonessential" business and all real estate activities shut down in that state for a couple months. Not every state went to that extreme, but you can see that no one knew the nuances of this time in history and how it would affect them.

You have no idea what outside forces will attack your business. You have no idea if there will be another global pandemic or when the stock market will fall or when the housing market will crash again. You have no idea if the city, county, or state that you live in will change some rule or law dictating the way you do business or change the way your company operates. There are a multitude of factors and forces that affect your business that you do not think about or wouldn't even think you'd need to think about.

This is why you need reserves in at least the **Profit** and **Owner's Tax** accounts. Reserves are not only for peace of mind, but to cover the practicalities of external forces that you don't even know how to prepare for. It's also to help cover if you make a mistake in business or run into an obstacle.

Reserves are like having insurance on your business. You may not see the need for insurance at the time of purchase, but when you *do* need it, you are more than glad that you've paid for it. When, *not* if, you run into a difficult time in your business, you will be very happy that you built reserves for your company.

Building reserves also provides peace of mind for your family. Wouldn't it be great if you could tell your family that you have several months' cash reserves in the bank for your business and could weather a storm instead of always being uptight about the funds? Wouldn't that give your significant other some peace of mind that you don't live deal to deal? Right now, they might ask you about your business, and you say that you know you currently have deals to close, so the money is okay. Or maybe you avoid talking about the business or money like the plague because you have no earthly idea where you stand. That's why being able to view the health of your business from your bank accounts is so important. You can look at the accounts and know quickly the temperature of your business, and it will empower you to be able to have intelligent conversations about your business with your family.

WHICH ACCOUNTS SHOULD ACCUMULATE RESERVES?

"I received a huge *six figure* tax bill and started panicking. I had no idea what to do," Joe McCall told me as I interviewed him for this book.

He explained, "At the beginning of my investing career, I was the jack of all trades and the master of none. I felt like I spun my wheels but got nowhere in my real estate business. When the crash in the late 2000s happened, I lost a lot of money in the recession and it almost took me out of the game. I sought help at the time to get back on my feet and someone suggested at a mastermind I attended that I read *The Pumpkin Plan* by Mike Michalowicz, and that book really hit home."

In that book, Mike talks about mastering the one thing you're good at and defining who your customer is. Joe started to really think about who his customer was and came to the conclusion that the people he should focus on were his buyers. He needed to tailor the deals to their needs. "After focusing on my buyers, my business started to explode."

Joe started to make a ton of money in real estate. For several years, he also had a ton of tax write-offs because of all the losses he had sustained during the recession. He had more write-offs because he and his wife had adopted four children. This guy is the real deal, as you can see. After several years, the write-offs from his losses ran out.

He told me, "I was slapped with the huge six-figure tax bill. I panicked because even though I made a lot of money through real estate, I didn't have six figures sitting around to pay my taxes. I was caught with my pants around my ankles and my head buried in the sand. I had no idea what to do, and I was flustered and frustrated all the time."

At this point, he knew he needed help but didn't know what to do. Thankfully, he still went to masterminds and was around good people who he had built relationships with over the years, and he heard other investors recommend *Profit First*.

Joe said to me, "The system sounded great, but initially I didn't think I could do it. I knew I needed help though, so I went out and found a bookkeeper to help me get my finances in order and to help me implement Profit First inside my business. That person helped me so much. I kicked myself for not hiring someone sooner to help with my finances. She helped keep me accountable and not spend the money in the Profit or Owner's Tax account. I made sure to have an Owner's Tax account set up to pay my current tax bill and to pay down the six-figure bill."

"The IRS doesn't care about how old you are, what you do, or anything like that," Joe said. "They care how much you owe them. A lot of my friends told me they were in the exact situation as I was and needed help too. I was very surprised to find out a lot of other investors were in the same boat when it came to taxes, but it was a relief to know I wasn't alone. I knew that not saving for the IRS or managing the money was a big issue for almost every owner. I have been able to save for taxes and pay down my old tax bills. I'm so glad I set up the tax account."

I want you to have the same peace as Joe. You will have to pay the IRS unless you have a lot of rentals and take every tax break you can or lose money year after year in your business. More than likely, you will pay something in taxes. You may have never saved for taxes before in your life and may always be stressed around tax time.

The **Owner's Tax** account is one of the three main accounts for which I want you to hold reserves:

- **Profit** account

  This account should be the first account you transfer money into. The **Profit** account is about a return on the money, time, and energy you've invested to start and run the business. This one should steadily build a reserve.

- **Owner's Tax** account

  The **Owner's Tax** account can pay the quarterly taxes for the business if that is how you pay taxes currently and can also be used to pay your taxes when you file your personal tax return. Uncle Sam will get his money. I am not saying you shouldn't do everything in your power to use every tax advantage out there to lessen your tax burden, but you should have that **Owner's Tax** account set up, fund it, and *not* spend the money in there except to pay taxes.

  A quick tip about the **Owner's Tax** account: If you end up saving too much money for taxes in a year, you can transfer the excess amount to the **Profit** account as a bonus for yourself.

- **Emergency** account

  I recommend you have at least one account dedicated to emergencies. Whether it be a global pandemic, a key employee quitting, a change in government regulation, or anything that may throw your business for a loop, you will be glad to have an **Emergency** account. I suggest keeping at least three months' worth of operating expenses in this account. Alternatively, you can have every account hold more than one month's worth of reserves. If you do this, you will have extra in the **Profit**,

Owner's Comp, **Owner's Tax**, and **Operating Expense** accounts. That means if you have a slow month, you can still pay yourself and run the business. Some investors we work with want three months of operating expenses in their **Operating Expense** account at all times for the peace of mind to be able to weather a bad quarter.

HOW DO I KEEP MYSELF FROM SPENDING THE RESERVES?

As long as there have been human beings on planet Earth there has been temptation. I face it on a daily basis. There's always too much good-tasting stuff to eat at the house because my wife is an amazing dessert maker. (Yeesh, now I'm thinking about cookies. *Must. Resist. Temptation.*) If the yummy food sits in front of me, the temptation is a lot stronger than if I have to go to the store to buy the junk food.

What about work as the temptation? Does your work tempt you when you should be with your family or playing with your kids? I can get sucked into working too much and have to schedule my time and be held accountable to make sure I prioritize the right things. Not all temptation is evil. But it can lead you down the path to losing what really matters.

It's the same with your finances. You will begin stockpiling cash in your bank accounts as you run Profit First. You will save for your taxes throughout the year now instead of waiting until the last possible second to do a deal to pay your taxes. You will build up money in a **Profit** account. You *will* be tempted to take that cash all the time from those different accounts if you stare at it every day.

If you constantly raid these accounts, you know that the business is not where it should be, and it will force you to take a hard look at where you are. These accounts are in place to help you have peace of mind, grow as a business, and to save your behind at tax time.

Do not raid your reserves!

Let's get to what you care about: How do you make it harder to spend the money that will accumulate?

1. Set up the **Profit** and **Owner's Tax** account as savings accounts at a different bank.

   In *Profit First,* Mike suggests setting up two new savings accounts for the **Profit** and **Owner's Tax** account at a completely different bank and to make it as hard as possible to access that money. I am all for this if you are a one man/woman operation or if you're just starting out and don't have anyone to hold you accountable. Every time you do your allocations, you move the money for the **Profit** and **Owner's Tax** to the savings accounts at the other bank and "forget" about them until every quarter is over.

2. Set up the **Profit** and **Owner's Tax** account as savings accounts at the same bank, but put them on a different login than your other accounts.

   I give credit to real estate investor Paul Thompson for the idea behind this suggestion. Most investors log into one account to view their money, so if you have a completely different login and password for the accounts you shouldn't touch, I guarantee you won't look at them as often and you've taken a huge step in helping yourself be disciplined enough to not spend the money constantly. As a real estate investor, this is probably a better option than separate banks.

3. Use accountability partners.

If you have people on your team who help you with your finances, make sure to have them hold you accountable to not spend the money in the **Profit** and **Owner's Tax** accounts. You can hire a fractional CFO or tell your bookkeeper or accountant to hold you accountable and call you out whenever they see money spent other than for paying taxes or taking a profit distribution once a quarter.

Joe McCall made one such hire to help hold him accountable to these principles and to make sure he had enough to pay himself and cover his tax bills. He told me, "Hiring someone for accountability was one of the best investments I made because it keeps me on track with my finances and keeps me accountable to put the money away for taxes."

The important part of this whole chapter is to make sure you do whatever works for you, so that you can stay away from the money that is truly not yours. You will save yourself a lot of pain, stress, worry, and heartache by keeping money in those accounts. You bring stability to your company, your employees, your family, and yourself by making sure you have money in the accounts when you need them.

WHEN CAN I SPEND MY RESERVES?

The **Profit** account and **Owner's Tax** account will sit and accumulate money, so when do you use the money from those accounts? Let's go over the accounts individually.

I've seen investors use the **Profit** account for different purposes such as debt paydown, a reserves account, or straight profit. All those purposes are great! The whole point of the system is to accomplish the goals that work for your business.

I've worked with a lot of investors who want to pay down bad debt and use the **Profit** account as their debt pay-down account. They keep a certain amount in this account (anywhere from $1,000 to $5,000) to make sure they still have profit available, but use the rest of the funds to pay down debt.

If you don't use the **Profit** account for debt paydown, every quarter, reward yourself by taking out a percentage of the profit. I'd suggest taking anywhere from 10% to 50% every quarter because you may also use this account as your reserves or emergency fund, and I understand not wanting to drain the account. But *do* take something out of the account because you need that tangible reward for building a profitable business. Make sure to use this money you take out for you and your family or for whatever is important to *you!* The **Operating Expense** account should sustain the business, so the **Profit** account should be for whatever you want to spend your profit on.

The **Owner's Tax** account is simple. If you pay quarterly taxes for the business, the funds come from this account. When you pay your personal taxes would be the other time to use the funds in the **Owner's Tax** account. Please heed the Joe McCall story and don't touch this account so you can build up a tax reserve. This brings tremendous peace of mind and saves you from scrambling every year at tax time.

If you do set up an **Emergency** account, please plan on what constitutes an emergency and use the money for those purposes *only.* If you take money out of the **Emergency** account other than for the preplanned scenarios, you cripple your business and weaken your system. This is a good way to stay in the rat race.

Please hear my plea on keeping extra money in the accounts. You will be able to make more money without doing more deals just by keeping reserves. Those extra funds will give you a sense of peace and clarity to help make decisions and will help you be bankable to private and institutional lenders. Reserves and profitability are the best ways to grow your business, not by raiding your accounts and "reinvesting" every dollar.

START NOW

1. Commit to profitable growth by giving yourself permission to hold money in reserves.

2. Choose one of the suggestions to hide the money from yourself that needs to be held in reserves.
   a. Set up the accounts at a different bank
   b. Set up a different login for the **Profit** and **Owner's Tax** accounts
   c. Hire a Profit First professional to hold you accountable to the system and to remove temptation.

3. Plan your next Profit draw and put it on your calendar to celebrate your profitability!

Chapter 7

LEVERAGE YOUR BOOKS TO GET THE MAXIMUM BENEFITS

Knowing your numbers is not just about getting off the deal-to-deal rollercoaster. Knowing your numbers can put substantial amounts of money in your pocket—immediately.

I started working with Rich Lennon, the investor whom I mentioned earlier, several years ago. When I first went to work with him, he mentioned that he had built his business like a battleship and "reinvested" all his profits back into this business to help it grow. When I hear this now, I know this is almost always real estate investor code for "I don't know my numbers or what I'm spending, so I throw every dollar back into my business to cover my ever-increasing expenses." To be fair to Rich, he did build his business like a battleship and had a fair amount of reserves. He also wanted to reinvest into his business with more clarity. That's not the typical investor situation, however, as I know after analyzing hundreds of companies and talking with as many investors.

When I dug into his books, I realized right away that the person who entered Rich's data did so incorrectly and, as a result, Rich couldn't get the numbers he needed. It took several months to get his books into shape. Once that happened, a light bulb went off for Rich. He now knew his monthly expenses to the penny. He now knew how much he had put into a property at the drop of a hat.

With his newfound clarity, we could see that the debt on his portfolio was about 38%, and he was underleveraged. He had a lot of his own money in his rentals, and he didn't want that. He was able to go to a bank armed with his financials and request a refinance of his portfolio. He ended up receiving several hundred thousand dollars of his money back. On top of all of that, this happened right at the beginning of the COVID-19 pandemic. He now had over a year's worth of reserves in cash and had options while other people panicked.

Rich also put in place a person specifically on his team to report to him every week on every single dollar that came in and went out in cash. This was another huge benefit to him because he now had the pulse of the business on a week-by-week basis. He has been able to make decisions at a moment's notice because of the power he now has in his hands. He restructured his business several times because of what his numbers told him.

Do your books need rehabbing? Can you look at your books from a high level and see if your financial statements make sense? If you own a flip property and you're halfway through the rehab, does the amount shown on the balance sheet of that property make sense to you?

If there are numbers on your P&L and balance sheet that don't make sense and your bookkeeper can't explain them to you, it's time to look for a new bookkeeper. Not having the right numbers will really cripple your business; it's like running a marathon with a broken leg. Confusion about your books brings stress and poor decision-making. Clarity brings confidence and the ability to make better decisions. You've busted your hump for your deals. Don't you want to keep the money you earned?

Knowing your numbers could send you on a guilt-free vacation.

Knowing your numbers could get you several hundred thousand dollars in your pocket immediately.

Knowing your numbers could be the difference between keeping your doors open or not.

Knowing your numbers will be the difference in you making and keeping more money in your pocket instead of sending it all out the door.

Knowing your numbers will keep your lender's money safe.

Knowing your numbers will give you the power to change your business and ultimately change your life.

In this chapter, I give you the knowledge you need to unlock all of the benefits I just mentioned. With this knowledge, you can run an in-depth Profit First assessment on your business, leverage your numbers to get a better return on your marketing, know the difference between a project budget and a company budget, and take more steps that will help you keep more of the money you make without doing more deals.

Let's get to what you care about: how to get your numbers in order to leverage them.

HOW TO GET YOUR NUMBERS IN ORDER

1. Hire a competent financial team.

As real estate investors, we know the power of every dollar and we want to save and get discounts everywhere we can. I marvel at the deals we can make happen. This mentality can create a problem when it comes to choosing your financial team. A lot of investors look at hiring a bookkeeper, CPA, or

CFO as a needless expense because they don't see the immediate payoff compared to hiring a salesperson who brings in deals.

In the previous paragraphs I listed the tangible rewards of knowing your numbers. If you have a financial team who is competent, they will be able to give you all those benefits. They're an investment to your business and not just an expense.

Do not focus on discounts when it comes to the financial team. The cheapest option is usually never the best option. You may have hired a virtual assistant to do your books, but do you know if they've been inputting your data correctly? Can you hold them accountable? A good financial team will guide you to be able to hold them accountable and show you the numbers in a way you understand to let you make informed decisions.

A bookkeeper, CFO, and CPA are the components of a powerhouse team.

The bookkeeper is like the nurse of the business. They come in and check on you constantly and make sure your numbers are in order. They don't prescribe anything. They input transactions and run your payroll and do the nitty-gritty tasks. A great bookkeeper will have the books in order on a weekly basis or at a minimum biweekly so you can use the financial statements such as the P&L and balance sheet to make decisions. They hand you those reports, but don't go over them with you.

The CFO is like the doctor for the business in the sense that they help with the overall health and wealth of your company. They come in every so often to look at your numbers and tell you how to get better. They are always on the lookout to make sure you stay healthy and give you the advice you need. The CFO is there to help grow your business and make sure you don't blow apart while you scale. They are the people on the team who sit at the same level as you and help guide and make decisions that affect the company. They are the ones who take the financial statements, help you make decisions, and recommend courses of action for you to take. They also could be the ones who implement Profit First in your business and help you get your mind wrapped around your finances in a simple way.

The CPA is like the specialist. You go to a specialist when you need a specific area covered that the bookkeeper or CFO don't handle. They handle taxes, and great ones can help you save a lot of money and can be a vital part of your team.

All these people should help you make and keep more money. Their job is to handle the finances and give you the confidence to make decisions based on hard numbers and not on a whim. As you grow, your financial team will grow too. Most people think of scaling their sales, marketing, and operations teams, but most do not think of scaling their finance team. This is a huge mistake. As you grow, you'll need that finance team around you to make sure you are on top of every number in your business to get the most benefits out of the business and to save your butt from hot water.

As Rich grew his company, he added each one of these roles to his company. He has a bookkeeper to help him input his data, a CFO to help guide him in the big decisions of the finances, and a CPA to get the best tax benefits possible. His financial team helped him pocket hundreds of thousands of dollars.

2. Have your financial team run a complete analysis of your financial situation.

After you have a great team in place, have them run an analysis on your financial situation. When we onboard a new client at our company, Simple CFO Solutions, we run an analysis on the overall systems, processes, and the current state of the books. Then we tell our investor clients what it will take to get their books up to standard.

You'll need someone to be very honest with you about where you stand. You may need to invest a couple thousand dollars to get your numbers up to date or clean up the mess left behind by a bad bookkeeper. This is why it's important to not neglect the financial aspect of your business. The longer you wait to get everything in order, the more cleanup will be needed.

A true business owner thinks of every area of their business and makes sure they have competent people in place.

3. Be prepared to help your financial team get your numbers in order.

Once you have a professional assessment of your business financials and a recommended course of action, be ready to give your team whatever they need to help you. If I haven't beat this into your head already, your numbers can help take your business to where you want to go and beyond, so do what is necessary to get in that position. This may mean you need to help gather documents and have several meetings with the financial team to help clean up the mess. A good financial team will ask the pertinent questions and help streamline this process, but they will still need direction and input on your end.

What's great about this process is that when you have the books caught up and in order, maintaining them should not take as long. Now, you'll have the numbers you need to help your business grow and put more money in your pocket.

WHAT DO MY NUMBERS MEAN?

The title of this section is the rallying cry of all real estate investors everywhere when they are presented with numbers by their accountants or bookkeepers. So many investors we work with say that when they get reports or financial statements from their bookkeeper, they have no idea what the numbers mean let alone what they should do with the information presented to them.

I want to give you the power to understand your financial statements. I do not want you to feel stuck, alone, or frustrated anymore because you don't know how to read the statements. You are not alone when it comes to not being able to read these reports. Just because someone might be doing more deals than you are currently does not mean they have it all together.

For example, I worked with a client recently who made over seven figures in his real estate investing business, and he said, "I have no idea how to read any of the statements. I just do the deals and get them done and hope there's enough money in the account next month."

If you feel apprehensive about learning the basic financial statements, do not worry. I do not go on and on about everything you do not need to know. This next section is short and to the point to get the data you need as the business owner. Leave the in-depth analysis to your numbers people.

In order to equip you and make you feel empowered, I want to give an overview of the financial statements. Knowing the basics will help you implement the PFREI system and run the PFREI Assessment. I'm going to tell you where real estate related items sit on these specific reports. I'll also give you some examples of the different financial statements for your reference.

If you want to take your financial statement knowledge to the next level, I *highly* recommend picking up Dawn Fotopulos's book, *Accounting for the Numberphobic.* It should be required reading for every business. Dawn paints vivid word pictures that make all of the statements very easy to understand.

Here is a great example from her book: "Your financial dashboard has three gauges you need to be able to read to manage a business—your Net Income Statement, your Cash Flow Statement, and your Balance Sheet. These statements measure the vital signs of your business operations. They provide you with critical information about how much profit the business is generating, how much cash you have in the bank to run the business, and the overall health of the business at a point in time—information that allows you to make wise and timely decisions that will keep the business humming like a tuned-up car."

Let's review the main financial statements.

THE PROFIT AND LOSS STATEMENT (P&L)

Even if you aren't sure what all of the numbers on it mean, you are probably familiar with the profit and loss statement (P&L), also known as the income statement. Your P&L covers a specific period of time, such as a previous week, month, quarter, or year. You can compare prior quarters and years and gain great insight by tracking the profitability trends.

You need to understand your P&L because it tells you how much you make every month, how much you spend every month, and if you run at a profit or a loss. The business's expenses show up on the P&L, and that tells you how much you need to make in order to cover the operating expenses.

I recommend you look at the P&L at least every thirty days to see where your business stands. In real estate you might have a negative month because the house closings are pushed back or the rent all came in the days before or after the current month.

As long as you have strong, profitable quarters, a slower month will not kill you and put you out of business. If you have a bad quarter or several bad quarters in a row, you are on the quick decline to a painful business death. Knowing your financial health and the profitability of your business will help you pivot or tell you you're on the right track.

Another big benefit of the P&L is the ability to track your marketing expenses, which sit on this statement. Knowing how much you spend per marketing channel will be a huge bonus to you because then you can track how much money it takes to bring in leads from different marketing channels. Break those bad boys down into Direct Mail, Facebook, PPC, and so on.

Let's learn how to read the P&L. There are three main categories.

1. Income
2. Cost of Goods Sold (COGS)
3. Expenses

The top two categories when combined (income *minus* COGS) give you your gross profit. All three categories combined give you your net Profit (income *minus* COGS *minus* expenses). Pretty simple to follow, right?

In any finance software you use, you will have what is called a chart of accounts. This is like the category fields you may have in your CRM (Customer Relationship Manager) system to manage your leads. It tells your data where to sit on the financial statements, so you can pull the proper reports.

Let's get to what you care about: Real Estate Investing categories related to the P&L.

EXAMPLES OF INCOME ACCOUNTS:

1. House Sale Income (main account)
   a. Wholesale income
   b. Assignment fee income
   c. Fix-and-flip income
   d. Turnkey income

2. Rental Income
3. Owner Finance Income

Examples of COGS/Pass Through Revenue Accounts:

1. Cost of Sales (main account)
   a. Wholesale COGS
   b. Assignment fee COGS
   c. Fix-and-flip COGS
   d. Turnkey COGS
   e. Closing Costs COGS
   f. Interest COGS
   g. Holding Costs COGS

Examples of Expense accounts:

1. Admin Expense
2. Advertising/Marketing
   a. Facebook
   b. Direct mail
   c. Referrals
   d. Search engine optimization (SEO)
   e. PPC
   f. Any other marketing source you have
3. Automobiles
4. Charitable Contributions
5. Cleaning

6. Commissions
7. Depreciation Expense
8. Dues and Subscriptions
9. Gifts
10. Interest Expense
11. Management Fees
12. Meals and Entertainment
13. Office Equipment
14. Payroll Expenses
15. Professional Fees
16. Property Tax Expense
17. Rent Expenses
18. Training/Education
19. Travel Expenses

This is not a comprehensive list of accounts, but it gives you a good example of the kind of accounts that sit on the P&L. You may need to add more, and you can figure that out by looking at your statement. If you don't have numbers in the income portion but you know you sold properties, you know you are probably missing data. If you look at an expense item and something is way too high or way too low, bring that up to your bookkeeper and ask them about the line items to see if they miscategorized transactions to the wrong account. If you see categories on the P&L that start with the words "Uncategorized" or "Suspense," that means those transactions have not been placed in the proper account yet and you need to get your bookkeeper the details of those transactions. These accounts would show up in any software you use because they are "catch all" buckets for transactions that are not categorized. Those would be the main points I'd be looking for when looking at a P&L.

SELLING COMPANY
Profit and Loss Statement
January 1 – December 31, 2021

INCOME

Income Assignments	$90,000.00
Billable Expense Income	$4,000.00
Credit Card Cash Rewards	$3,000.00
Interest Income	$3,000.00
Property Sales	$10,100,000.00
Total Income	$10,200,000.00

COST OF GOODS SOLD

Property Rehab Costs

Property Maintenance (COGS)	$10,000.00
Subcontractor Labor (COGS)	$1,300,000.00
Supplies & Materials (COGS)	$90,000.00
Total Property Rehab Costs	$1,400,000.00

Property Sale Costs

Assignment Fee (COGS)	$20,000.00
Closing Costs (COGS)	$880,000.00
HOA & Other Fees (COGS)	$5,000.00
Inspection Costs (COGS)	$20,000.00
Interest Paid (COGS)	$225,000.00
Photography (COGS)	$5,000.00
Property Insurance (COGS)	$45,000.00
Property Tax (COGS)	$50,000.00

Bonus Tip for the P&L

Make sure your bookkeeper is using Classes in QuickBooks Online or whatever software you're using. Classes are another category feature. For every single transaction tied to a property, that property should be selected as the class. Why do you care about this? Because if you tie every related transaction to a property, you can pull a P&L per property! This is so important because it tells you what you actually make per property and gives you the data

Purchase Costs (COGS)	$5,025,000.00
Utilities (COGS)	$25,000.00
Total Property Sale Costs	$6,300,000.00
Total Cost of Goods Sold	**$7,700,000.00**
GROSS PROFIT	**$2,500,000.00**
EXPENSES	
Advertising & Marketing	$300,000.00
Bank Charges & Fees	$4,500.00
Education	$7,500.00
Happy Company Employee Fee	$43,000.00
Interest Expense (revolving)	$500.00
Legal & Professional Services	$32,000.00
Meals & Entertainment	$2,000.00
Office Supplies & Software	$33,000.00
Other Business Expenses	$250.00
Pete's Car & Truck	$10,000.00
Postage & Delivery	$150.00
Rent & Lease	$12,000.00
Repairs & Maintenance	$4,000.00
Taxes & Licenses	$600.00
Travel	$7,000.00
Uncategorized Expenses	$500.00
Utilities	$3,000.00
Worksite Employee Payroll	$240,000.00
Total Expenses	$700,000.00
Net Operating income	**$1,800,000.00**
Net Income	**$1,800,000.00**

you need to be able to make changes in your business.

Here is an example: You make a purchase of materials for a fix-and-flip project at 123 Main Street. In your finance software, there will be a category field called "Class" where you can enter in the property address "123 Main Street" and tag that material purchase to that property. You can assign a class for any transaction tied to that specific property. Then you can pull a report by the class and be able to see how much you've spent so far. When you sell the

CATEGORY	DESCRIPTION	AMOUNT	CLASS
House Purchase: 123 Main Street (Flip)	Flooring Labor Costs for 123 Main Street	450.00	123 Main Street (Flip)

property, you will be able to pull that property's specific profit and loss. It will look something like the example above.

BALANCE SHEET

Ah, the balance sheet. One of the most misunderstood financial statements in the real estate investing world. This statement is easy to understand, *if* you have been taught how to read it. I will make it easy for you to read now.

The balance sheet tells you in a nutshell what you own (Assets), what you owe (Liabilities), and the balance between them (Equity). Lenders want to see if your Assets (cash on hand, properties, land, and so on) can cover all the Liabilities (credit cards, mortgages, private loans, any debt, and so on), and then some.

If you can read the balance sheet and you have someone entering in your data correctly, it will tell you which properties you're currently flipping and how much you are "into" them such as purchase price + repairs + holding costs + any other cost = total "into" number. The balance sheet will tell you how much you've borrowed against each property and how much of your lender's funds you have left to spend on a property before dipping into your own. For example, say you borrow $150,000 for the purchase and rehab of a house. The house price is $100,000 and for the rehab you estimate $50,000. Say you go over budget and end up spending $60,000 on the rehab. On the balance sheet for the property (the asset), it would show $160,000 that you are "into" that property. The loan (the liability) you have on the books would be $150,000. This tells you that you have put $10,000 of your own money into that project. Do that too many times without getting proper funding or watching your rehab budget and you can get into a cash crunch really quickly. See why the balance sheet is so important?

The balance sheet is also different in how it measures time. It is a snapshot in time versus a time period like the P&L. Whatever the end date you set for the balance sheet, it shows the account balances as of that date.

Again, there are three main categories on the balance sheet; Assets (what you own), Liabilities (what you owe), and Equity. Pretty simple right? Let me give you examples of what is included in those categories as they relates to real estate investing.

Examples of Asset accounts
1. Bank Accounts
2. Flip Properties (while they are under rehab)
   - Break each property into a subcategory below the main account.
   - If you rehab more than one hundred properties a year, you might want to run everything off classes and not break down each property as a sub account.
3. Rental Properties
   - Break each property into a subcategory below the main account.
4. Land
   - Break each property into a subcategory below the main account.
5. Accounts Receivable (such as invoices out to tenants)
6. Notes Receivable (such as when you sell a property on seller financing)
   - Break each property into a subcategory below the main account.
7. Vehicles Owned by the Company

Examples of Liability accounts
1. Credit Card Accounts
   - Break each card down into a subcategory.
2. Lines of Credit
3. Long-Term Mortgages
   - Break down by property secured by
4. Short-Term Private Loans
   - Break these down by lender
   - Can also break them down by house

SELLING COMPANY
Balance Sheet
January 1 – December 31, 2021

ASSETS
Current Assets
Bank Accounts
  Primary Bank - Bank of America

001 Income	900.00
002 OPM	25,000.00
003 Profit	30,000.00
004 Owners Comp	15,000.00
005 Owner's Tax	20,000.00
006 OpEx	40,000.00
007 Reserve	30,000.00
008 Investors Reserve	7,000.00
Total Primary Bank - Bank of America	$167,900.00
Total Bank Accounts	$167,900.00
Accounts Receivable	0.00
Total Accounts Receivable	$0.00

Other Current Assets
Note Receivable

Note Receivable - John Smith 1234 Main Street	17,000.00
Note Receivable - Jane Doe 5678 Profit Road	18,000.00
Note Receivable - Roger Cruz 990 Cashflow Ave	29,000.00
Total Note Receivable	$64,000.00

Examples of Equity accounts

1. Owner Draws (if you take money out of the company that isn't part of a set salary)
2. Owner Investment (if you put capital into your business)
3. Retained earnings (what your company has made as net profit in previous years)
4. Net income (shows the net income of the P&L for the date you select)

Rehab Properties	
8765 Main Street	155,000.00
2345 Timothy Road	135,000.00
7878 Catalpa Ave	78,100.00
Total Rehab Properties	$368,100.00
Total Other Current Assets	$432,100.00
TOTAL ASSETS	**$600,000.00**
LIABILITIES AND EQUITY	
Liabilities	
Current Liabilities	
Credit Cards	
Business Credit Card - 7575	20,000.00
Total Credit Cards	$20,000.00
Property Loans	
8765 Main Street Loan	170,000.00
2345 Timothy Road Loan	110,000.00
7878 Catalpa Ave Loan	100,000.00
Total Propery Loans	$380,000.00
Total Liabilities	$400,000.00
Equity	
Retained Earnings	30,000.00
Shareholder Distributions	-130,000.00
Net Income	300,000.00
Total Equity	$200,000.00
TOTAL LIABILITIES AND EQUITY	**$600,000.00**

I kept this explanation high-level because it's truly what you need to know from this statement for the purpose of this book. We could delve deeper into the balance sheet, but then you'd be bored to tears. Hopefully this overview at least helps you understand more and see the balance sheet in a simpler way.

Where to Find the Profit First Numbers on the Balance Sheet

If you take an owner's draw in the place of a salary or in addition to your salary, that will show up on the balance sheet in the Equity section. This will be an important number to run the PFREI Assessment.

Also, if you hold rentals and pay long-term mortgages on the properties, the principal payments for those mortgages are included in the Liabilities section of the balance sheet. The principal payments will be important numbers when you run your PFREI reports.

CASH FLOW STATEMENT

You know that cash is important. You know that cash gives you the power to buy houses, pay yourself, pay employees, pay for systems, and invest. Then it stands to reason that running *out* of cash is a terrible thing. Everyone I've ever read about the subject of cash in your business equates it to blood. Mike Michalowicz says, "Cash is the lifeblood of your business." The *why* of your business is like your heart telling the blood where to go, but without blood, there is no purpose for the heart. Without cash, there is no way to accomplish your vision and the purpose of your company.

The cash flow statement or statement of cash flows tells you where your actual cash is moving in your business during specific time periods. This financial statement is actually really simple: It

	OCT 2021	NOV 2021	DEC 2021	TOTAL
SELLING COMPANY Statement of Cash Flows October – December, 2021				
OPERATING ACTIVITIES				
Net Income	200,000.00	325,000.00	200,000.00	$725,000.00
Adjustments to reconcile Net Income to Net Cash provided by Operations	-55,000.00	25,000.00	-5,000.00	-$35,000.00
Net cash provided by operating activities	$145,000.00	350,000.00	$195,000.00	$690,000.00
INVESTING ACTIVITIES	-$30,000.00	-$50,000.00	$40,000.00	-$120,000.00
FINANCING ACTIVITIES	$90,000.00	130,000.00	$10,000.00	$230,000.00
Net cash provided by financing acitities	$60,000.00	$80,000.00	-$30,000.00	$110,000.00
NET CASH INCREASE FOR PERIOD	$205,000.00	$430,000.00	$165,000.00	$800,000.00

shows you the net increase or decrease of your cash in your company. You can increase or decrease cash from operating activities (the income and expense of your business and the loans you've taken on properties), investing activities (such as the buying and improving of properties), and financing activities (owner's draws or taking cash out of the business). If your books are up to date and accurate, you can pull different time periods to see how your cash has fluctuated.

I will say that the PFREI assessment and system helps you understand your cash from the owner's perspective better than the cash flow statement, so that's why I am not spending much time on it.

> "Cash is to your business as blood is to your body. The definition of bankruptcy is running out of cash—not net revenue, not profits, but cash. Managing cash is mission critical to keeping a small business alive. Cash is like fuel in your car—it's what keeps your business running. Cash pays all the expenses."
> Dawn Fotopulos, *Accounting for the Numberphobic: A Survival Guide for Small Business Owners*

YOU HAVE YOUR NUMBERS IN ORDER, NOW WHAT?

Getting your numbers in order puts you into a whole new category, lightyears ahead of other investors. Now, you can get the maximum benefit from your business.

Let's get to what you care about: What are actionable items you can do with your numbers?

1. Run a PFREI assessment.

After you have your numbers, you can run an in-depth assessment of your business. This assessment is different than the instant assessment we talked about in Chapter 3. The instant assessment gave you a quick snapshot of where you are, and you only needed rough numbers of what you made, kept, and spent. The in-depth assessment is important because it takes in the actual numbers from your business over a period of time and gives you more concrete percentages. You can figure out exactly what you made, paid yourself, and spent on your business in any given time frame. This helps you set your CAPs and TAPs more accurately. Why is this important? You will have a clearer picture of where you are (CAPs) and can fine-tune your percentages, so you can move toward your goal percentages (TAPs).

I originally wrote eighteen pages of a step-by-step walkthrough of running an assessment on a selling or buy and hold business, but I *know* you. You'd flip through the pages and see if you'd want to run it, or more likely you'd avoid running the assessment because it's too much work or you're scared of the outcome. If you've read the whole book to this point, you may be the 5% of investors that will walk through the step-by-step process of running your own assessment, so I've included several ways to run it:

- Flip to the PFREI Assessments in the back of this book for a step-by-step walk-through.
- Go to simplecfosolutions.com/pfrei to download the assessment and watch a video tutorial.
- Go to simplecfosolutions.com to learn about how our company can do an assessment on your business for you.

2. Get the maximum return on your marketing dollars.

This benefit might be the most exciting to you. After you have your numbers in order, you will be able to clearly see the dollar amounts you spend on each marketing channel. You will also know how much you've made on each property individually so you can now match the property to its acquisition source and get the return on investment.

Say you sold four properties and made a total of $40,000. Because you know your numbers, you can see that all of your deals came from leads generated through direct mail, and it cost you $8,000 dollars to get those four deals. Your return for that lead source would be five times what you spent, which is good. This is how you build KPIs (Key Performance Indicators) that tell you which channels work and which ones do not—and should be cut.

I've worked with investors who have their numbers in order, and when we put together all their returns on their marketing channels, they clearly saw which of their marketing channels gave them a return on their investment. This is how you can use your numbers to make and keep more money without doing more deals. It's playing the game smarter to get the maximum benefits from each lead source, fueled by your numbers.

3. Know your "into" number at any time.

Your "into" number is how much you have currently spent on a property at any given time. If you pick up a rehab property for $50,000 on the books it will show $50,000 in that property's asset account. As you spend money on the rehab, the dollar amount shown on that asset account will increase so you will know how much you are "into" the property at all times.

Knowing your "into" number is very powerful. This number helps you determine budgets for your projects. To be clear, a project budget is different than a business budget. A project budget accounts for a specific house and how much you intend to spend before selling or renting the property. A business budget takes into account the total income and expenses of the business. I know it may sound simple, but a lot of investors don't know the difference.

If you secured a private lender for the deal and begin to go over budget, you might use your own money to cover the overage because you got just enough funds from the lender to cover purchase plus your projected budget for the property.

For example, if the lender gave you $100,000 and you spend $50,000 on the purchase and the rehab ends up being $60,000, your "into" number on this property is $110,000. You had to use $10,000 of your own money to cover this project. Do that more than once and you start digging a deeper hole. When you don't know your numbers, you may not realize you're in the hole at all and wonder why you never have any money in your accounts.

Let me tell you another quick story from Joey English. A Zoom call I had with him changed both our lives.

Joey sat in his office grinning from ear to ear.

"Why do you have that big goofy grin on your face?" I asked.

"I know that when we get on calls that there is always going to be something new to learn, so I'm excited for the call."

I then asked him a question he'd never been asked before: "How much are the properties in your portfolio worth?"

"I don't know, I just think about rents coming in, vacancy rates, taxes, insurance, and cash flow, and haven't thought about an overall perspective like that."

Joey ran market values on each one of his properties and totaled all the values. He discovered he owned real estate valued at $1.9 million. He came back and showed me all the total of all his properties.

"That's pretty cool, Joey."

"Yeah it is. I've never thought to look at it like this."

"You know what else is amazing? Your mortgages only represent 32% of the total value of your properties. Do you know what that means? It means you have more than a million dollars in equity in your portfolio."

Joey sat there stunned and then said, "Okay, I'm trying to absorb this."

"You're a millionaire, my friend!"

"I'm a millionaire?! I'm a millionaire!"

Joey hurried home from his office right away and went through the numbers I showed him with his wife, Ashley. He revealed to her that they had more than $1 million dollars in equity and told her, "Ashley, we're millionaires!"

She told him, "That's amazing! I don't feel any different though."

Joey responded, "Neither do I, but isn't it cool to know? It gives us security that we have such low debt on our portfolio. We've also come a long way from losing our shirts."

You may be a millionaire like Joey, but if you don't know your property "into" numbers, you will remain in the dark. Or you may be like Rich and have a lot of equity and want to re-finance to pull cash out. If you don't have a clear picture, you won't be able to gain those benefits.

START NOW

Your numbers will help you grow your business and get the maximum benefits from it. The clearer you are on your finances, the easier it will be to make better decisions that will ultimately help you make and keep more money without doing more deal volume. The goal of this chapter has been to kick you in the butt to get serious about your numbers in a holistic sense.

Here are the practical steps I suggest you take:

1. Take stock of your financial team and see if you need to

    upgrade or train them to get your books up to date.

2. Hire someone to run a full PFREI assessment.

3. Set up KPIs around your marketing dollar returns.

Chapter 8

HOW TO MESS UP PROFIT FIRST FOR REAL ESTATE INVESTING

G etting to Chapter 8 in any book, let alone a nonfiction business book, is an accomplishment for anyone, so I want to commend you for getting this far.

PFREI involves opening up the bank accounts, figuring out your Need number, transferring the income, building and holding reserves, running due diligence on your business, making sure you have the proper books and numbers in place, and managing your finances as a whole. That's a lot. I get it if you feel like you're drinking from a firehose and need to take a breather.

At this point, you may feel a tad bit overwhelmed or you may think, *PFREI sounds great, but my company is different, so I can't implement it.* Has that line of thinking helped you up to this point? Has that thinking helped you close more deals or make more profit? I know there are actions to take, and it will take some time to get this system up and running. The time you invest in this system is worth every second because every single second you spend on implementing PFREI in your business will pay dividends.

"I can't possibly implement this system. I have way too many accounts and entities already, so how could this system possibly help me?" This is what Tim Davis told me when we first started working together.

Tim was in the same boat as a lot of the clients who come to us who have no idea where they stand financially. He thought he was profitable because more money came in than went out. He reached out to us because he wanted to see exactly where he stood.

Tim started his own business when he was twenty-five and never looked back. Some of the businesses didn't make it, and he had to start over again. He learned a lot from the school of hard knocks along the way until he was able to sell his construction company. He still has a property management company, a fix-and-flip company, a lending company, and his own rental portfolio.

All of these companies and entities were already a little overwhelming, and the thought of adding PFREI with more bank accounts gave Tim hives. He thought he would need to open six more accounts per entity, resulting in over thirty new bank accounts.

In a meeting with Tim, I had to ask questions of my own, such as, "With all of the bank accounts you have now, do you have clarity on your finances? Do you know where you stand as far as your books are concerned because your current accounts don't give clarity?"

In both cases, Tim's answer was a resounding, "No."

Tim knew there was a problem. The problem wasn't a revenue issue. The problem was he didn't know where all of his money was and where it went.

PFREI is about gaining financial clarity in the most efficient way possible. I've outlined the steps in this book, but the system needs to work for you and not against you. Meaning, if you can see yourself in Tim's scenario, or if your situation is unique in a different way, customize the system for your business.

For Tim, we outlined a plan to implement PFREI in a way that would fit his businesses. Instead of opening thirty new bank accounts, we ran the assessment on each entity. Seeing this high-level view of his companies was truly a light bulb moment for Tim. I'll never forget in one of our meetings, he repeated over and over again, "This is so cool."

Just as he suspected, Tim's companies were profitable overall, and now he had the numbers to back him up. We then had him open the "Golden Trio," but not for each entity. Tim used these as master accounts into which all of his other entities transferred revenue. He still followed the core steps of the system but *adapted* them to his process and business.

You don't have to follow Tim's approach. We have other clients with multiple entities who *do* open the accounts for each one.

This is why I love PFREI. It's not about opening the bank accounts or running transfers; it's about building successful habits and realizing the full benefits of your business.

I wanted to tell you about how we implemented PFREI for Tim because initially he was reluctant to do it. For the rest of this chapter, I will show you the common objections and fears that I hear over and over again. If you've been skeptical up to this point, I want to break down some of those mental barriers in your head so you can live the life through real estate investing that you've always wanted to live.

Let's dive into what you care about: how to mess up the system.

THIS SYSTEM IS NOT FOR ME

Thinking that this system is not for you is more of a mindset objection than a factual objection. If you think you can't implement the system, you are right. The Henry Ford quote, "Whether or not you think you can, you're right" is used all the time, but it definitely applies to how you view PFREI.

You may think, *This system sounds great, but I can't possibly implement it because my company is too new, or too big, or has too many accounts already, or it sounds like a lot of work.* If you want to end up like every real estate investor who doesn't have a system and who is stressed to the max, loses sleep at night, isn't able to grow the company and replace themselves, and never achieve true financial freedom, by all means do not use PFREI. My point is that your mindset is the biggest barrier to starting and maintaining this system.

If you need help with your mindset, I highly recommend the book *Can't Hurt Me* by Navy SEAL David Goggins. It's a real kick in the pants and will help you unlock the barriers in your mind to not moving toward the goals you have.

I suggest this book on mindset for you because we *all* struggle in this area. I remember when I first started my company, I often wondered, *Why would people want to listen to me?* I struggled with thoughts like, *I'm not good enough to run a business,* or *There are other people who know finances better, so why try?* That internal dialogue can be so damaging, and it definitely did a number on me. I'd wake up every morning with a sharp pain in my stomach because I was so worried about providing value and making sure I truly helped people. It turns out after meeting with companies, implementing PFREI, and helping real estate investors gain clarity, I realized that I had always provided value but my mindset and self-doubt caused havoc.

The key to overcoming self-limiting beliefs and self-doubts is to take action. Doubting yourself and worrying does no good. Prove to yourself that you are good enough and that you *can* do what you set your mind to do. Taking action is what helps me move forward every single day, no matter what my mindset is.

This system is for every real estate investor who wants to run their company like a true business owner. If you can't get over the barrier of your own mind, you will struggle with a lot more than just your money management. I implore you to *take action!* Open one bank account, get yourself on payroll, but please do *something.*

DO I REALLY NEED ALL THESE BANK ACCOUNTS?

As a real estate investor, you may already have a lot of bank accounts. You may have opened bank accounts for each new property you acquired at the beginning of your investing journey. I've worked with several real estate investors who were exactly in this position. They already had a lot of bank accounts, but the bank accounts did not give them clarity regarding the health of their business. Most still had one main account through which they ran most transactions, and it was a mess.

The point of the system is *not* just to open bank accounts, but to help you manage the money and see the health of the business at a glance. If you have a thousand bank accounts already but aren't clear on your business's health, you still need the foundational accounts. You need to separate out your **Profit, Owner's Comp, Owner's Tax, Operating Expense,** and **Other People's Money** to gain a clear picture of your business.

Often, you'll have accounts that you haven't touched for a long time because a project or house is done, and you didn't repurpose the account. Now would be the time to repurpose some of those accounts to be foundational PFREI accounts.

I do want to address that if you don't have a lot of bank accounts already and are skeptical of opening the foundational accounts, please open at least two new ones: the **Profit** account and the **Other People's Money** account. Take baby steps. Separating your Profit and the money that is not yours will help you a lot right away, so I highly encourage you to at least open those accounts.

I interviewed Pace Morby, the "Subject to" king, on my PFREI podcast. He mentioned that anytime he starts a new business, he builds the foundation on Profit First. He told me during that interview, "If I had Profit First implemented in the first business I started years ago, I'd have five million dollars more in my bank accounts right now."

YOU KNOW YOU'RE NOT PROFITABLE

I worked with another client (who will remain nameless). When we helped them know where they stood with their numbers, had their books clean, and ran an assessment on the business, they discovered they were very much in the red. They knew they had big problems, but up to this point, they didn't know just how bad the problems were. They lived on borrowed money and time. They thought that they couldn't implement PFREI because of how far in the hole they were.

PFREI works no matter your situation. The whole system helped them figure out just how far in the red they were and helped them start identifying the expenses they should cut with the P, R, and U expense cutting system I talked about earlier in the book. They also identified what would get them back in the black and projected what a profitable month would look like.

The system is not just about the assessment, setting up the accounts, or the transfers. It's a culmination of the system as a whole. Whatever piece of PFREI you can use right now to help your business get back on the right track is what you need to use. Even if you are in the red, you can still run allocations because this will force you to see what comes in and goes out on a consistent basis. If anything, you need PFREI more when you are in the red because it will force you to look at those numbers and get out of the hole as quickly as possible.

The alternative is to keep your head in the sand, stay in the red, and eventually have to fire everyone and close up shop. PFREI can save you from all of this because it forces you to take action where you are and keeps you on top of the business.

I JUST WANT TO DO WHAT I'VE ALWAYS DONE

I'm sure you've heard this saying before: Doing the same things you've always done and expecting a different result is the definition of insanity. As a fellow real estate investor, I definitely understand being a little insane. But if you keep your head buried and don't manage your money, you won't get a different result. If you struggle in your business and are stressed to the max, something needs to change. If you are successful in your real estate business but think you could do better, something needs to change. If you have no idea where your money goes, something needs to change. If you are tired of the up-and-down cycle of the cash flow in your business, something needs to change. If you don't pay yourself what you need and it brings stress to you or your family, something needs to change.

Please do not keep killing yourself and stay in the "grind" or the "hustle" without thinking about the health of yourself and your business. You cannot run the business as you have been and expect different results without changing what you do. Trust me when I say PFREI will give you those different results.

I understand that PFREI isn't a marketing system or a selling system or something that might sound sexier to you. But it *is* a system that helps you make and keep more of your money. The sexy part is being able to live without stress and be financially free. So please, for the love of God, commit to doing something different in your business so you can get a different and *better* result!

I NEED TO GET THIS SYSTEM JUST RIGHT

I have worked with several clients who, in an effort to get it just right, analyzed the system to death and made it way more complicated than it needed to be. Investors overcomplicate PFREI by thinking they need to be hitting their TAPs (Target Allocation Percentages) right away, which can effectively kill the business instead of helping you work slowly toward the goal.

One of the easiest ways to overcomplicate things is to overthink the CAPs when you first start. Being able to see where you've been can really help you determine your starting point, but if you aren't able to easily get your numbers, start with easy, doable percentages. If that means you transfer 1% to the **Profit** account, that's okay. If that means you think you need to start your **Operating Expense** account at 95%, that's okay. You need to start where you are *now*, and then become better over time and move closer to your specific TAPs.

It's very easy to overcomplicate and overthink any system, and PFREI is no different. I implore you to take those first couple steps. Open the bank accounts, allocate the funds, and start where you *are* and with what *you* can do.

I DON'T WANT MY LENDERS TO KNOW MY NUMBERS

I know your secret shame. If you've seen the movie *Fever Pitch,* you might remember the scene where Jimmy Fallon, who plays a teacher in the movie, takes his high school class to an office, where they meet a data analyst, played by Drew Barrymore. She tells the kids that some people take numbers, rearrange them in their heads, and put them in more interesting patterns. One of the kids says, "She knows my secret shame," because he does the nerdy thing she describes.

Unlike in the movie, the problem in your business isn't a cute nerdy problem. It's a real threat to your business, family, and reputation. You might be in a situation where you don't make money and use your private lenders' funds to float your operations. This is a dangerous place to find yourself.

You were so excited. You had your first private money lender for a project to rehab. You had the best intentions to use the funds to purchase the property, fix it up, and hold it until it sold. *But* you ran into problems with the rehab budget that you didn't foresee. You have one bank account holding all your funds, so you saw the amount get lower and lower and started to panic. You went out and found another private lender for your next property, but used those new funds to pay the rest of the current project and the Ponzi scheme began. You never intended for this to happen, but it did. What's worse, you may not even know you dipped into the new private lender's funds for your old rehab because you had no idea where you stood financially.

So what do you do if this happens? Do you reach out to the private lender and tell them the situation and see if there is more equity or room to fund the overage in the rehab? Do you take a step back and see where you stand financially and if you can float the overage on the rehabs yourself? No, you are unaware of the problem until it is way too late and your cash and the lender's is almost gone. So you go to another private lender and get more funds for another deal and start in the hole from the last deal with the last private lender, and you use the new private lender's funds for the other rehab and get further and further in the hole financially until you struggle to pay back the deals and the lenders when they eventually sell.

I won't say that you will never go over on a rehab or that you won't ever find yourself in a cash crunch. But I will say that you need to know where you stand financially, and you need to make it as easy as possible on yourself to know your cash positions. You need a system that helps you manage your cash and even more importantly helps manage the cash of those who have trusted you with *their* funds.

You have a very deep responsibility to your private lenders. I interviewed David Phelps, the owner of Freedom Founders, a group of dentists who lend to real estate investors. David was a dentist for years and invested in real estate to help escape the rat race. He also has been lending privately to real estate investors for years and started Freedom Founders to help other professionals obtain financial freedom outside of their dental practice.

David has seen every situation happen in the private lending world. He has had deals go sideways, not get paid back, and real estate investors go dark on him. He told me, "No one intends for a deal to fall apart from the beginning. Every investor should have a backup plan for when situations arise that aren't ideal. The worst thing possible an investor can do is hide when things go wrong."

He posted on Facebook about the moral and ethical responsibility of real estate investors to their lenders because he had a friend he'd known for more than thirty years run into a bad situation on his investments and suddenly go dark. There are some great points in this post, which he permitted me to include in this book:

[Warning – Rant]

Somewhere in the teachings of the great real estate creative genius gurus was missed one important point:

"When you use, take, borrow or otherwise create joint ventures with other people's money ("OPM"—a favorite guru buzzword), you not only have a legal responsibility to that person (or entity), but a moral one as well.

"But David, it's all about non-recourse, no personal liability, asset-layered protected deals!" "That's what they teach us... right?" "That way, you can't ever get into trouble."

Not so fast, grasshopper.

It's a small world that we play in. We often use words like, "relationship capital," "financial friends," "your network is your net worth."

And then comes the day of reckoning. It happens with every business cycle.

As Warren Buffett says, "You find out who's been swimming naked when the tide goes out."

"Everyone's a genius in an up-market."

There have been a lot of skinny dippers jumping in the water in the last six years as we moved toward the end of the great bull market.

It's not a pretty sight as the tide is going out quickly now.

I invest just like any other investor—with eyes wide open. There is risk. Big boys and girls understand that.

I often invest with or through other people (network, relationship capital). That is a choice.

The vast majority are people who hold true to their word (it's called "integrity"). But there will always be a minority in every population group who have a greater self-interest and behave by a different set of rules.

So, what's the point?

This isn't being harsh or throwing stones to those who find themselves in difficult times during this unprecedented pandemic. Stuff happens. It's life.

But, if you borrow, take, or use other people's money with a written agreement as to how that money is to be paid back and you find yourself in a position, whether by your neglect or not, that you can no longer abide by those promises, YOUR MORAL AND ETHICAL OBLIGATION IS TO COMMUNICATE!

I am appalled (and you would be too if you knew the names, which I will not disclose) of those who have reneged on promises to pay and fail to communicate. They go "dark."

Suddenly, the very person who was "your financial friend" and for whom you provided capital for deals within hours of the request goes into hibernation.

The lesson here is, don't run from your obligations.

Stand up. If something goes wrong and the deal isn't working or something happens in your business or personal life, communicate! Let the other party know what's happening and what your plan going forward will be.

That's honor. That's integrity.

Never make a lender or joint venture partner have to come find you and ask what's going on!

I've worked with people in the past who out of complacency, bad management, bad records, a bad market or other extenuating circumstances, had to work themselves out of "the hole." Sometimes it takes more than a couple of years, but they don't run from their obligations.

These are people I will generally do business with again. I can trust them to follow through no matter what.

Please don't misconstrue the message. I'm speaking about a minority. Most people with whom I have conducted business I have long-term relationships and will continue to enjoy doing business with. That's fun! And everyone benefits!

The few who disappoint—it's their choice, it's on them. But I will never do business with them again nor could I recommend them to anyone else.

Remember: It's a small world and you can't buy back your reputation once it is tarnished.

Bottom line: If you don't intend to honor your word, don't involve yourself with other people's money or assets.

And please, don't teach "your model" to other people!

Rant over."[2]

After reading David's words, I think the picture is clear that you have a deep moral obligation to do everything in your power to help private lenders not only feel safe lending to you but to protect their money with every fiber of your being.

I also asked David about PFREI and if that bore any effect on an investor getting a loan. He told me, "If an investor tells me they have a system like PFREI in place, I know they care about their cash flow and don't fly by the seat of their pants. It goes a long way in my due diligence on that investor."

In this book, you have learned how to manage other people's money and not only make the lenders feel safe but also put a system in place to set off warning bells for issues with your cash flow and your private lender funds. You do not have to find yourself in a Ponzi scheme any more after you implement the steps of this book.

ROBBING FROM YOURSELF TO FUND YOURSELF

In the spirit of being open with your investors, you need to be open with yourself. If you have multiple entities, you may already play the money shuffle game, but after you open multiple

---

[2] David Phelps. Facebook, May 17, 2020. https://www.facebook.com/groups/realestateinvestorsuccess/permalink/3116033311787013/.

bank accounts, you will be very tempted to move funds all the time if you do not have the proper mindset. A lot of REIs who have multiple entities take the cash they need from one entity to cover the cash flow issues of another business instead of addressing the reason for their cash flow issues head on. This is what Joey did with his rental entity and his flipping entity. He would cover the losses and expenses from his flipping entity with the cash flow from his rentals. Until he worked with us, this habit of stealing from himself taught him that it was okay to not address the root issues of his flipping company. Using the PFREI system helped Joey understand the root issues and stopped the intercompany transfers to cover his cash flow problems.

After you set up all the accounts, whether you have one entity or dozens, you will be tempted to move money from one account to another. I implore you not to steal from the different accounts. The whole system is about discipline, putting yourself in a better position, growing your wealth, and making better decisions. Forcing yourself to not steal from your accounts for any reason builds the discipline of good financial management and also forces you to make better decisions. Don't have enough money in your **OpEx** or House Purchase account for that deal that just came along? Where can you get the money to take down the deal? What contingencies do you have in place to capitalize on opportunities when your cash is low?

What about if you overspend on a project? Do you take the money straight from the **OpEx** account, which will now throw off the cash for your monthly expenses? Most people don't think when it comes to their money.

Do *not* put a Band-Aid on your finances when you need surgery. This book can help you perform corrective surgery on your thought patterns to optimize your business's finances. Ask yourself better questions.

I DON'T HAVE ENOUGH TIME TO DO THIS

Have you ever been near a Jimmy John's when they run their $1 sandwich special? There is a line out the door that circles around the building several times. People will wait for over an hour and sometimes more just to get a $1 sandwich and save a couple dollars. I get wanting to save money, but if you step over $100 bills to pick up pennies, your perspective on time and money needs to shift.

If you don't think you can implement PFREI because you don't have the time, you undervalue your time. The return on investment and time is one of the greatest ROIs you can have in your business when you set up this system.

Profit First also really puts into perspective how much you are worth according to your business. Remember how we've spent so much time making sure you pay yourself and figure out what to pay yourself from the business? Now that you have an account dedicated to **Owner's Comp**, you will see very clearly what your business thinks your value is.

At the beginning of this chapter, I talked about feeling overwhelmed, and I know it can be daunting to do something you've never done before. I know one of the objections you may have is that there are too many things to do and maintain, and you already have so little time because you work so much in your business already. If this is you, I highly recommend the book *Clockwork* by Mike Michalowicz. It tells you how to streamline the other areas of your business as well.

Thinking you don't have enough time is still a mindset issue because this system will save you time, headache, heartache, and money. It saves you time because you now have a streamlined system to manage your finances, pay bills, and complete other tasks more efficiently. It saves you headaches because your finances will become a monster if they are not managed properly.

It saves you heartaches because you can prevent your business from going belly up and you can make sure your family is taken care of. It saves you money because it forces you to know where your money comes from and where it goes.

As I said before, PFREI has a great ROI because you set up the system and then reap all these benefits over and over again for years.

I CAN'T START RIGHT NOW

The worst way to mess up PFREI is to not start now when you have the step-by-step process of how to implement the system inside of your business. Earlier in this chapter, I shared a quote from Pace Morby who told me if he had started this system when he first started investing, he would have $5 million dollars more in his bank account today. He is *not* the only investor I interviewed who said they wish they would have had this system sooner because it has saved them so much time, sanity, and money.

Wherever you are in your investing journey, now is the time to start the PFREI system. If you are just beginning, I'm excited for you because you can start on the right foot in an area that most investors avoided because they didn't have a book like this to guide them. If you are in the middle of your investing journey, now is the time to stop living deal to deal, being stressed about your finances, and losing out on profit that you've already made. Starting this system will transform your business and will transform your life, so why would you wait to start? This system will add more zeros to your business than you could have imagined. Are you ready to take action?

START NOW

I hope this chapter has helped you see that the biggest ways you can mess up Profit First are by not starting the system now, overcomplicating the system, and having the wrong mindset when it comes to implementing the system. Please take some time and follow these action steps to help you.

1. Sit down and think about whether any of these points in this chapter are holding you back from starting the system. Pinpoint which ones resonate the most with you and commit that you won't let those objections stop you.

2. Do something! The best way to break your current mindset is to take some sort of action. Set up a bank account or reach out to a Profit First implementer, but do something that moves you in the right direction.

3. Start the system. If you haven't started the process up to this point or haven't opened a new bank account, please go out right now and set up at *least* one new account.

Chapter 9

HOW TO USE PROFIT FIRST REI TO ATTRACT BETTER DEALS, PRIVATE LENDERS, AND OTHER BENEFITS

I f you turned to this chapter because the chapter title intrigued you, read on because this one (just like every other chapter *cough cough*) can change your life. If you have read the whole book up to this point, you are an amazing human being, and I want to thank you for sticking with me.

I want to give you specific ways to use PFREI to take your business to the next level above and beyond financial management. This is a jam-packed chapter of information to use to transform your business into the powerhouse you've always wanted your business to be.

USING PROFIT FIRST REI TO SECURE MORE PROFITABLE DEALS

PFREI uses percentages to ensure the health of your business. You can use this same line of thinking to analyze your deals to make sure that your properties are "healthy" deals and not the slim margins that you sometimes take because you need another house.

If you remember, we talked about your Need number in Chapter 2, and we dove in deep about how to find the profit you needed to make in order to pay yourself. In this section, it's all about the ways to make sure that the deal is a healthy deal.

At this point, you should be able to run an assessment on your business and know the profitability of your company. Knowing how much profit you make per deal will unlock a whole lot of other information you can use to your advantage.

If you are a BatchSkipTracing user (they help you with lists, skip tracing, and a whole host of other services), you may know their motto: Data is king (and queen!). By implementing PFREI, you now have data that will tell you exactly what you need to know in order to make better deals. Your finance software is truly the CRM for your money and contains so much of this data that can help take you to the next level. In Chapter 3, we talked about splitting out your marketing costs into different subcategories in your software. This is so important because now you can track certain numbers that make a huge difference in your business.

I would highly recommend tracking total profit, average profit, and number of deals sold per acquisition/marketing method, disposition method, and location. I'd also track overall profit per month, quarter, and year. This will give you so much relevant data to help operate the business at a totally different level.

If you can track these numbers, you can tell right away which deals are the most profitable for you by acquisition method, disposition method, and by location. Do you see the incredible power this puts into your hands? You can now identify the specific acquisition and disposition methods and locations you and your company should focus on to grow the business profitability. Maybe even more importantly, this data will tell you what to *stop* doing in order to be more profitable. By knowing what deals are the most profitable and bringing in the most money for you, you can devote your time and attention to truly the highest returns on your time.

I remember when we first showed Dan, the investor from the introduction, his data from his sold properties. This was after he was open to more data about his properties. We showed him the profit per acquisition and exit strategy. It blew him away because he realized, in the year he lost money, his profit per flip was abysmal compared to his profit per wholesale deal.

Dan was just like other investors and just like you in that he wanted to squeeze every single dollar from every deal that he could, so when a property would come along, he'd guess how much he could make on a wholesale or a fix-and-flip and sometimes ended up choosing to fix the property and sell it at retail. Dan's core focus and genius, however, is wholesaling, but he got caught up in the "squeezing more juice from every lemon" syndrome that permeates the real estate investing world. Don't get me wrong, I'm all for fixing and flipping and capturing every dollar out of every deal, but not at the cost of losing time and money and ultimately your business.

Dan always thought that the flips would yield more bottom-line profit, but he never had hard numbers to back up that assumption. When we gave him the numbers, it turns out that his profit per fix-and-flip was half of his wholesale deals and about twice the headache. This was one of the key light bulb moments for Dan that helped him turn his business around. He thought before that he had to fix-and-flip to make more money when in reality, he had to stay in his core business and focus on doing the deals that would bring him the most profitability. If your core focus is fixing and flipping, go all in and get every process in place to ensure max profit per deal.

Having the power of these numbers in your hand can change you from beating your head against the wall over every deal to having a consistent stream of deals that will make you more profitable. You might say, "That sounds great but how do I actually track all of this?" If you go to simplecfosolutions.com/pfrei, you will find a video of how we track these numbers and how to use the data.

USING PROFIT FIRST REI TO BRING IN THE PRIVATE LENDERS

Using PFREI to bring in private lenders is one of the most exciting parts of the system because, as a real estate investor, you will want or need private money at some point to take down deals to either rehab or hold. So many investors want to know all the secrets of attracting private lenders and think that it's some big mystery. There is *no* mystery or big reveal.

Real talk for a second: If you are not managing your current finances at all or well, why would anyone want to invest in or with you? Let that sink in for a second. I know it hurts, but you need to hear this. *If you don't manage your finances currently, you do not deserve private money.* Your numbers, the health of your company, and your profitability is sacred, but the money you borrow from private lenders should be respected and revered and the lenders *need* to know you view their funds in that manner. That is the true secret to finding and keeping private lenders.

If you have a track record of good deals, you are already well on your way to attracting private lenders because money always looks for a place to be put to good use. If you add that you manage your finances well, you have the winning combination.

The best way I can illustrate this is a conversation I had with David Phelps, who you might recall from Chapter 8 is a private lender and the founder of a private lender mastermind, Freedom Founders. I have great respect for David. He cares about his members, and he cares about who they invest with. To be considered to offer deals to his group, investors must go through his rigorous screening process. He doesn't just have a virtual screening process; he flies to wherever the investor operates and vets the leaders at the company. He asks himself, *"How do they run the company and who is their team?"* In that way, he can make sure his members are protected.

If you remember, I asked David if running Profit First would help an investor's cause for being able to offer deals to his group. He resoundingly said, "Yes!"

PFREI will not only help manage your business finances, but also help you prove to private lenders that their money is secure. Not every private lender has a screening process like David Phelps does, but you still need to give your lenders as much reason to trust you as possible. Telling those lenders that you run on PFREI and that you have a separate bank account specifically for private lenders' money will give them peace, and help build trust. It shows the lender that you care about them and that you care about their finances and care enough to have a system to make sure they will be taken care of even if the deal goes sideways.

The next time you talk with a private lender about a deal, tell them that you run on the PFREI system, which means that you have a process to make sure they get paid back and their money is used for the intended purpose every single time. Also, if you think they might take more convincing, you can show them your company's assessment and show them the health of your business. That exhibits competency and demonstrates that you look at your business overall in addition to vetting deals.

If you were on the fence about setting up the **OPM** account, I hope you see the power that account and the PFREI system brings to your relationships with private lenders. Protect their funds and show that you care about them, and you will always have the money you need for the deals you acquire.

USING PROFIT FIRST REI TO KEEP YOUR TEAM TOGETHER

I want to touch again briefly on how PFREI can ensure you have the funds and profitability to keep your team together and moving forward. We started working with a client who had a big team in place. The owner was very conscientious about taking care of his employees and wanted to pay them above industry standard. He fought long and hard to get his company profitable and a lot of his employees had been on that journey for a long time too. We met and showed him where the percentages could go to bump up the pay of the employees, and he began to increase their salaries. PFREI principles brought clarity to the owner, and it brought peace, stability, and happiness to the employees. Do you think that those employees are motivated to give their best and to be loyal to the owner when he has a system in place to make sure they are taken care of?

People will always be the number one investment in the business. Notice how I didn't call them an "asset" or an "expense." Your people are an investment. When I say investment, I mean a couple different things:

1. They are human beings who should be treated as such, and have goals, dreams, and aspirations like you do.
2. Every dollar you pay them should come back to you several times over.

Knowing you want to take care of them goes a very long way with your employees. The other side of the coin is making sure that every employee is worth the investment and time. Having the wrong people in place is one area that can really hurt your business. That's why doing the P, R, U expense exercise from Chapter 5 is valuable: It forces you to see which employees are profitable for the company and which ones may need to be replaced.

Another quick tip I want to give you regarding employees is when you pay them a bonus, make sure the company is profitable. Set up another account and put a percentage in that account to pay bonuses or give employees bonuses based on a percentage of the **Profit** account. That way, they can see that the more profitable the company is, the higher their bonus will be.

USING PROFIT FIRST REI TO PAY DOWN BAD AND GOOD DEBT

Real estate investing uses debt. Unless you are strictly assigning contracts and that's all you do your whole life, you will at some point touch debt in your business. Debt is a tool just like money is a tool. Make sure you have the right kind of debt in your business. (Dave Ramsey will probably hate me for all time for saying this.) Mike Michalowicz explained the different types of debt in a business, and I think his explanation is clear:

1. **Debt Leveraging:** This is the use of debt for high probability returns. You buy a house to fix-and-flip and then contact your private lender to finance the deal. They fund it. This is an example of debt leveraging.
2. **Debt Bridging:** This is the use of debt to cover short-term cash flow dips. In your real estate investing business, this may be a line of credit to cover the overage on a rehab when you go over budget when you know

that you just need the funds until the sale closes. This can be risky and expensive if the property doesn't sell, so use debt bridging sparingly.

3. **Debt Anchoring:** This type of debt has no predicted return. At this point, you use debt to maintain operations. You use credit cards to fund your typical expenses instead of the profit from your deals. If you don't have profit from deals to cover the expenses and have to use credit cards to fund your operations, you know there is a big problem. It's not just credit cards either; this could be when you take a private money loan from an investor and use their money to fund your operations instead of funding the rehab. This is why having one bank account is so dangerous because then you can't see clearly at a glance if you're using funds that aren't yours for your operations.

Profit First can also be used as a very powerful tool to pay down debt. I want to define the difference between bad and good debt for your real estate business too:

1. **Bad Debt:** This is any debt that is *usually* not tied to a property, has very high interest rates, and isn't being used to bring a return back into the business. This could be credit cards, unsecured loans from private lenders, lines of credit that you have been using to float the operations of the business, or private loans that are tied to a property you can't sell. This debt is chipping away at your profitability month after month. This is the debt that can end up killing your business.

2. **Good Debt:** This is debt that is tied to your houses, whether short- or long-term, that will generate

more money or net worth for you. These are the typical loans you get on a fix-and-flip or rental property. These loans should end up giving you a return that is more than what you put into them. The money in your **OPM** account is usually good debt.

BAD DEBT PLAN

One of the best ways to use PFREI is to help you pay down bad debt. When you open up your bank accounts, you might want to consider a "debt pay down" account. Take some of the percentage normally allocated to the **Profit** account and use it to pay down debt. I would still allocate at minimum 1% to the **Profit** account. So if you normally allocate 10% to profit, put 9% toward the debt pay down account and 1% to profit.

After you have your books in shape, ask your bookkeeper for a list of all of your business debts and categorize them as either good or bad. Then list the bad debt from smallest balance to largest balance and start paying down the smallest debt. After the smallest debt is paid off, the next allocations go toward the next highest debt balance and so on until the debt is all wiped out.

The real trick is to keep the bad debt down after you've paid it all off. In the real estate investing world, you can pay down a ton of debt quickly when your business is profitable from this system. In order to stop spending on the credit cards, the best thing you could do is to remove temptation. Remove temptation to use the cards by closing your credit card accounts and committing to using the **Operating Expense** account to fund the operations of the business. If you stick to this plan, you can knock down a ton of debt. I know I keep bringing Dan up, but he's a poster child for a lot of these points. Within the first six months of him hanging up on me, he paid down more than six figures of debt using this plan. It works. You have to be consistent and allocate money to pay down the debt.

The bonus is that when you do pay off all of the bad debt, you can go back to allocating all those percentage points to profit!

GOOD DEBT PLAN

I know a lot of books talk about paying down your bad debt, but what about the good debt that is tied to your long-term rentals? If your goal is to increase cash flow and your net worth, the faster you can pay down the loans, the better. For anyone who lost any houses in the 2007–2009 crash, I'm sure if they have rentals today, they are more cautious about how much they leverage those properties. I know people personally who lost whole portfolios of properties, and they weren't even over-leveraged but had 50–75% loan to value of their houses.

You do *not* have to pay down the loans on your rentals if that is not the overall goal of your business, but if you do want to, set up a plan to pay down your good debt a lot like you paid down your bad debt.

List all of the rental properties and the loans tied to them and arrange the loan balances from lowest to highest balance. Then start allocating a percentage of all the income to paying down this debt if your overall plan includes having free and clear rentals in your portfolio. This takes the burden off of completely paying off a property and puts in place a systematic approach that you can use every week or month to pay down the debt on your portfolio.

Remember how Joey didn't pay himself from the flipping company and used his rentals to pay his living expenses? When he implemented PFREI, he was able to pay himself from the flipping company. He then paused the payments to himself from the rental company and used the money to pay down the mortgages on his rental portfolio. Joey is on his way to having a free and clear portfolio in three years or less!

Can you see the power of using the PFREI system? It puts action and a process behind any goal that includes making more money or paying down debt. You can use it to pay down the debt on your houses and cash flow even more. Isn't this system incredible?

ADVANCED ACCOUNTS

This section should cover any other situation, even if you still think you can't fit into the "box" of PFREI. If you want to take your business to a new level or, if you are a larger operation, you can separate out the accounts even further to give you a more accurate picture of where your money goes.

Here are some of the types of accounts I've seen real estate investors use:

PITI Account

PITI stands for Principal, Interest, Taxes, and Insurance. I know I talked about this in a previous chapter, but I wanted to touch on this account again. This account would be mainly for buy and hold investors who want to separate out their monthly mortgage payments along with property taxes and property insurance. Some pay their property taxes and insurance separately from their principal and interest payments and pay the taxes and insurance once or twice a year, so this account can help you save for the property taxes and insurance payments on every single property. Even if you don't send a full mortgage payment to a mortgage company, you put the payments away on a monthly basis that you will make anyway for the year. This brings great clarity to you on what money is yours in your account and what money is for PITI. Because the Real Revenue formula for a rental company is Rental Income – PITI = Real Revenue, this account will help you know what your true cash flow is for your rental portfolio overall and per property.

Marketing Account

Any type of real estate company you own, whether it is a fix-and-flip or rental company, could potentially have a marketing account. I've seen real estate investors who specifically set up an account to funnel their marketing dollars into, so they can clearly see what they spend every month for marketing *and* what they can spend. This marketing account makes it very easy to track what works in your marketing and what doesn't. Marketing dollars are the fuel that drive your business, so you need to make sure your engine is always able to run.

Payroll Account

If you have employees you pay on a regular basis, I'd consider opening an account specifically for payroll. This would serve several purposes.

1. It helps you have peace that you have enough to pay your people every single time.

2. If you need to hire someone, start adding the money you know you'll need to pay them into that account *before* you hire them to make sure you will be able to pay that new hire without it hurting your business.

Bonus Benefit: It lets your people know that you care about them and gives them peace of mind.

This account can help you plan your hiring and cash flow *before* you hire someone. So many real estate investors hire people when they think they need a body before planning what that means in terms of cash flow in the business. This account will help you see if your business is ready to add a new position before you hire someone. I am all for growing your company in as healthy a way possible. This account gives you a tangible way to know if you can grow and scale at a healthy pace.

Investors' Principal Account

The investors' principal account is specifically for any money you get from private lenders or hard money lenders that is *not* tied to a certain property. I've seen private lenders who fund real estate investing businesses during growth periods and give them funds to purchase properties, but those funds act more as a line of credit than as a specific loan on a single property. You should set up a different account for that money: You want to make sure that as it goes out, you are always paying back the principal. If the funds are spread out over several different properties, you need a way to track when those funds come back after the properties sell, and what better way to track that money than putting it in its own bank account? If several private lenders give you $500,000 to spend like a line of credit, you know that if none of that money is used, you should still have $500,000 in this account.

Investors' Interest Account

This account goes with the Investors' Principal account, but the difference is you also need to save the interest that you will pay these investors because you won't pay them per deal. You will usually pay interest on a monthly, quarterly, biannual, or annual basis, so this account should clearly show whether you save enough in interest every month to be able to pay these investors.

> **Quick tip:** If you have a lot of bank accounts already set up, I want you to ask yourself two questions:
> 1. Do they still serve a purpose?
> 2. If they don't, can I repurpose any of my current accounts to be PFREI accounts? You may be able to use what you currently have as some of these advanced or foundational accounts.

PROFIT FIRST REI AND YOUR VENDORS

If you work with realtors, contractors, or other investors, there are other Profit First books specifically for each of them. There's a *Profit First for Real Estate Agents* by Damon Yudichak, *Profit First for Contractors* by Shawn Van Dyke, and this book for your real estate investing friends. How cool would it be to give the vendors you work with a copy of a book that is tailored to them to make them more profitable? Do you think your vendors would respect you more if you showed that you cared about their business?

Giving your vendors these books shows that you want them to be profitable and don't want them stuck in their own rat race. This act of generosity will motivate them to perform better for you and gives them another reason to be loyal to you. Wouldn't it be great if your vendors didn't have to worry about the financial side of their business and had a system for it so they could focus more on your projects and taking care of your needs? This is a way to work with vendors, show you care, and potentially create a solid business relationship for life.

Go to simplecfosolutions.com/pfrei to see the order links for these books.

START NOW

This chapter was a lot of fun to write because Profit First is more than just bank accounts and accounting. It's a mindset and has more benefits than just making the management of your money simpler—but if that was all it did, it would still be a *huge* benefit to you and your business. You can use this system to attract private lenders, make better decisions on your deals, and give you peace of mind by having reserve accounts for when the storms come. I want to encourage you to use this system and all its benefits.

1. Set up a dashboard and track your deals' total and average profit by acquisition and exit strategy methods and by location to get a handle on your business and really operate like a true business owner. Go to simplecfosolutions.com/pfrei to get a template on how to track these KPIs.

2. After you have your accounts open, write down potential private lenders to contact on your next deal and tell them that you run on PFREI. Put a sentence in your Facebook posts when you sell a deal and talk about how you helped private lenders make money. Say something to the effect of, "We always keep every dollar secure that is lent to us by using the PFREI system."

3. Determine if there are any advanced accounts that you want to set up that fit *your* business. If you don't think you need any advanced accounts at this time, make sure you set up the foundational accounts.

4. Grab a copy of *Profit First for Real Estate Agents* by Damon Yudichak and *Profit First for Contractors* by Shawn Van Dyke and give one copy to one vendor this next week. See how it changes your relationship with them!

EPILOGUE

Eric was one of millions born in China in 1970. When he attended college in 1997, he heard Bill Gates speak about the internet and knew he wanted to come to America and start a company. Shortly after, he applied for a visa to come to the U.S. Over the period of about a year and a half, he was denied eight times! Thankfully, he persisted and on his ninth attempt, his visa was accepted.

When he came to America, he began working for a startup called WebEx and made a name for himself. After a few years, Cisco Systems bought WebEx and Eric became the vice president of engineering. He made really good money in this position but wanted to change the structure of a product WebEx offered, virtual conferencing. The current software was clunky and not user-friendly at all. He couldn't convince the current leaders to let him tackle this project, so he took a great risk and went out and started his own company in 2011, Saasbee.

Saasbee took on the virtual conferencing competition head on, including Skype, Google Hangouts, and Cisco. Everyone thought Eric was nuts. As he built his company, he focused on the system and processes that would make his solution the absolute best no matter what. He launched the first official product for video conferencing in 2012 after spending more than a year dedicated to making the software as user-friendly as possible. The video conferencing software was faster and easier to use than anything on the market and Eric's company expanded rapidly.

Near the beginning of the launch, Saasbee changed their name to Zoom. Yes, the Eric I've been talking about is Eric Yuan, the founder of Zoom. In 2015, the software exceeded five hundred million meeting minutes a month and by 2019 the monthly meeting minutes were over five billion.

When COVID-19 hit in 2020, Zoom expanded revenue from more than $300 million in 2019 to more than $2 billion in 2020. In a time when both small and large companies have closed their doors at an alarming rate, Zoom was able to capitalize when others struggled because of proper preparation, the right system, and dedication to their end goal.

Yuan persisted in his efforts to come to America. He took the chance to do something new with Zoom because he knew he could make the lives of others and ultimately his life better. His company had massive growth in a time when other businesses went down left and right.

PFREI can be the system that catapults you and your company to massive *profitable* growth, and it will take persistence. It's your preparation for a better tomorrow and your safety blanket for today. It means more profit in your pocket now without doing more deals. It gives you confidence and safety. No one could see the pandemic of 2020 coming, but those who had cash in their accounts from the PFREI system could sleep better at night knowing they had the reserves to weather the unknown.

My mission in life is to change the lives of one million real estate investors through the knowledge in this book. I've witnessed this system change the lives of real estate investors over and over again. Just like Dan Guerin, who has built a seven-figure *profitable* business; Joey English, who does fewer deals, makes more profit, and takes vacations with his **Profit** account; Pace Morby, who set up each new business with PFREI because he doesn't want to lose out on another $5 million; and Rich Lennon, who went into the pandemic of 2020 with over eight months of reserves, you can leverage this system to receive what financial freedom means to *you*.

You will gain confidence, clarity, joy, and your sanity when you implement this system. That's a promise. I practice what I preach. I use this system in my businesses. Not only am I profitable, but I have the confidence to make informed decisions and steer the companies where they should go. My wife had health issues in 2020 and through the **Profit** account in the company I was able to cover the expenses needed without worrying about the next bill in the mail. It helps me sleep better at night, and I've heard from no less than forty real estate investors these same words, "I sleep better at night knowing where my money is."

The best part about PFREI? You don't have to be a "numbers person" to make this work for you. You do *not* need to take courses on accounting, bookkeeping, or anything terrifying like that. You need to leverage what you already do: looking at your bank accounts to become more profitable.

I've shared a lot of concepts with you in this book, but if you don't do anything else than set up one account dedicated to profit, I consider *you* a success and this book a success. Making the mental shift to profitability and not volume of deals will change your life immediately. Put the one action step of opening the **Profit** account and transferring 1% of every sale or rental income and watch as you take action how profit becomes a habit. Do this and you will right away see more profit without doing more deals.

I've talked with and interviewed dozens of real estate investors, every one of whom has implemented the system and made it their own, has a business now that they are in control of, and more importantly, has true financial peace in their life. They don't wake up worried about their finances; they don't have the fights at home like they used to; they aren't embarrassed to be in a room of other real estate investors and talk about their business; they don't worry about paying for their kids' schooling, or dentist visits, or the million other things that children need (can I get a witness here?). Every investor that I have talked to has seen the power of the system work for them. No matter if they do one deal a year or 100 deals a year, every investor believes that this system is the missing piece for their business.

This is what the system can do for you. Just as Yuan started Zoom in the midst of other tech giants with their own software, step out on faith and know that PFREI can change your life. You can be different from all of the other investors who keep their head in the sand, feel fear and anxiety every day, feel lost in their business, and are not profitable. You can implement these principles and have the life you always dreamed of. Take the action steps and see the complete turnaround of your business and personal life. You *can* get out of the real estate rat race and take control of your destiny and stop spinning your wheels. I've seen it happen with so many investors. Are you ready to become one of them?

All you have to do is take your profit first.

Appendices

CONTINUE YOUR
PFREI JOURNEY

I shifted my focus from full-time real estate investing to help you, the real estate investor, sidestep the financial landmines I saw people step on over and over again. I have a true passion for the investing community and want resources for any level of real estate investor. To continue your PFREI journey, join the private group here: simplecfosolutions.com/pfrei.

QUICK START GUIDE

STEP 1

Internalize the formula
"Sales – Profit = Expenses"

STEP 2

Run the Profit First
Instant Assessment
(Chapter 3)

STEP 3

Set up the foundational
bank accounts
(Chapter 4)

STEP 4

Pick your rhythm
for transfers and allocations
(Chapter 5)

STEP 5

Assess your business
every quarter

Appendix 2

THE IN-DEPTH PROFIT FIRST REI ASSESSMENT

This is the in-depth assessment in case you'd like to run it on your own. You can reach out to us at Simple CFO Solutions if you'd like us to help guide you through this process.

In the words of the Albanian terrorist to Liam Neeson in the movie *Taken,* "Good luck."

ASSESSING A SELLING COMPANY

A1: Top Line Revenue

Total money you made this year *before* you paid any property, business, or office expenses:

Money you made from

- Selling your rehabbed properties
- Wholesaling properties
- Any other income for this entity (for example, consulting, bank rewards, and so on)

Top line revenue means revenue you made that's above all your costs.

If you sold fix-and-flip properties or properties that you bought, this line will be the sales prices *plus* any assignment income, or any other income you made.

Source: Profit and loss/income statement

Look for "Total Income"

A2: Pass Through Revenue

How much it costs you to

- Buy, keep, rehab and sell your properties
- Any other closing and holding costs for properties you are selling

This is the "all-in" cost for selling a property.

Breakdown:

- Buy the property = purchase price, closing costs to get property, commissions
- Rehab the property = materials, subcontractors
- Sell the property = closing costs, commissions, holding costs, and other expenses so you can sell it

Source: Profit and loss/income statement

Look for the line items in the Cost Of Goods Sold section that directly relate to the sale of a property.

PFREI ASSESSMENT FOR A SELLING COMPANY					
	Actual $	Actual %	PF%	PF$	Difference
Top Line Revenue	A1				
Pass Through Revenue	A2				
Real Revenue	A3	100%	100%		
Profit	A4	B4	C4	D4	E4
Owner's Comp	A5	B5	C5	D5	E5
Owner's Tax	A6	B6	C6	D6	E6
Operating Expenses	A7	B7	C7	D7	E7

A3: Real Revenue (actual dollar amount)

The dollar amount you sold a property for *minus* the all-in costs to sell that property.

Money you made from your properties *plus* other income (Top Line Revenue) *minus* money it cost you to buy, keep, rehab, and sell your properties *plus* costs to make your other income (Pass Through Revenue)

This is the money that is available to allocate to your Profit First accounts.

Formula:

TOP LINE REVENUE
- PASS THROUGH REVENUE

= REAL REVENUE

(or: A1 – A2 = A3)

A4: Profit (actual dollar amount)

This is the amount of cash you have left over after paying all your costs, expenses, Owner's Comp, and Owner's Tax. If you're currently running Profit First, this would include the money you've saved in the **Profit** account.

Formula:

REAL REVENUE
- TAXES FOR THE BUSINESS AND OWNER
- OPERATING EXPENSES

= PROFIT

A5: Owner's Comp (actual dollar amount)

This is what you took out of the business for yourself. Owners pay themselves in many ways. Here are some common ways to look for how you may have paid yourself.

- Owner's draws/disbursements
- Payroll
- Reimbursements

Sources:
Owner's draws/disbursements = balance sheet
Payroll = profit and loss/income statement
Reimbursements = profit and loss/income statement

A6: Owner's Tax (actual dollar amount)
This is the amount you paid or set aside for your business taxes or your personal taxes.

This money is for the IRS. It is the amount of tax money:

- Your entity *already* paid for business and/or owner taxes.
- Your entity set aside in the **Owner's Tax** account to pay your business and/or owner taxes.

This is *not* the property taxes related to purchasing, keeping, rehabbing, or selling properties to make you money. That is in Pass Through Revenue.
Source: Profit and loss/income statement—more than likely there won't be any entries because the business hasn't paid your taxes before.

A7: Operating Expenses (OpEx) (actual dollar amount)
Cost to run the business and office
Catch-all for all business expenses that are not related to you making money.

This number does *not* include what it costs to buy, keep, rehab, and sell your property. Those costs are in Pass Through Revenue.

In this case, OpEx does *not* include
- Owner's Comp
- Pass Through Revenue
- Tax (business or owner)

Source: Expenses = Profit and loss/income statement

B4 – B7: Current Percentages

Every cell here is a simple formula to get the percentages you are operating on currently. You will be dividing the Actual Dollar Amounts for the accounts by the Real Revenue number.

Formulas:

$$B4 = A4 \div A3$$
$$B5 = A5 \div A3$$
$$B6 = A6 \div A3$$
$$B7 = A7 \div A3$$

These percentages will immediately be able to tell you whether you are way off track as a business.

C4 – C7: PF % = the TAPs

These cells are going to be the TAPs based on your Real Revenue for a year. Pick the column (A, B, C, and so on) in the Target Allocation Percentages table that matches the size of your business and put those percentages in C4–C7.

Example: You have Real Revenue of $463,212.52 for the past year. Your cells would be:

$$C4 = 10\%$$
$$C5 = 35\%$$
$$C6 = 15\%$$
$$C7 = 40\%$$

You can now compare your actual percentages in cells B4–B7 to the TAPs in C4–C7 to see how close you are to being a healthy company.

D4 – D7: Profit First dollar amounts

These cells are where you put the amounts that you should be socking away into the respective accounts if you have been following Profit First. Or if you haven't implemented the system yet, they show you what you should have funded into accounts. These cells are a formula also. The Profit First Dollar Amounts are found by multiplying the Real Revenue *times* the TAPs.

Formula:

$$D4 = A3 \times C4$$
$$D5 = A3 \times C5$$
$$D6 = A3 \times C6$$
$$D7 = A3 \times C7$$

SELLING COMPANY TAPS						
	A	B	C	D	E	F
Annual Real Revenue Range	$0–$250K	$250–$500K	$500K–$1M	$1M–$5M	$5M–$10M	$10M–$50M
Real Revenue	100%	100%	100%	100%	100%	100%
Profit	5%	10%	15%	10%	15%	20%
Owner's Pay	50%	35%	20%	10%	5%	0%
Owner's Tax	15%	15%	15%	15%	15%	15%
Operating Expenses	30%	40%	50%	65%	65%	65%

After inserting the formulas, you now have the Profit First dollar amounts for the accounts based on the Real Revenue and TAPs.

E4 – E7: The Difference

These cells tell you the difference between the dollar amounts you actually had in the first column and what the Profit First dollar amounts should have been.

Formula:

$$E4 = A4 - D4$$
$$E5 = A5 - D5$$
$$E6 = A6 - D6$$
$$E7 = A7 - D7$$

If the number in the Difference cell is negative, you need to increase the amount that you put into that account or it shows you that you didn't save enough. Here's an example: If you've never run Profit First and never saved for taxes, Cell A6 (the actual **Owner's Tax** account) is $0. When you take $0 saved for taxes *minus* what you should have saved, which is in cell D6 (the Profit First dollar amount for Owner's Tax), E6 (the Difference) will be a negative number showing you how much you need to save for taxes.

If the number in the difference cell is positive, you should decrease the amount for that category. An example would be if your operating expenses in cell A7 are $225,000, but the Profit First dollar amount in cell D7 is showing that you should have spent $185,285. The difference is $39,715 in cell E7, showing you that you spent about $40,000 more than you should have.

The different cells are to show you the dollar amounts you should save in the accounts and to show you how much less (or potentially more) you should spend on the operating expenses of the business.

ASSESSING A RENTAL COMPANY

Now I want to go over if you have rentals and how to assess your business as a buy and hold investor.

A1: Top Line Revenue

This is the total rental income or creative financing income you made for the year. This number will be one of the easiest to find.

Source: Profit and loss/income statement

Look for "Total Income"

A2: Pass Through Revenue (Principal, Interest, Taxes, and Insurance)

PITI = how much you pay for your rental mortgage loans

- P = Principal Payment for rental loans
- I = Interest. Loan interest for rentals
- T = Property Taxes. Property taxes for your rentals *only* (not the business or personal taxes)
- I = Insurance payments for rentals

This one can be a little fun to dig into in your accounting software because the principal payments sit on your balance sheet and the interest, taxes, and insurance are usually on the profit and loss. A lot of the investors we work with, however, keep track of their monthly payments in total on a separate spreadsheet outside of their accounting software. This is a quick hack for knowing what your monthly PITI out the door is for every loan you have on your rental properties and an easier way to get the PITI numbers.

If you have interest-only loans, you will use the interest, taxes and insurance for those loans because there is no principal pay down. If you have free and clear properties, you will still use the taxes and insurance but you won't have any principal or interest payments. Even if your portfolio is totally free and clear, there will always be a number in this cell because you

PFREI ASSESSMENT FOR A RENTAL COMPANY					
	Actual $	Actual %	PF%	PF$	Difference
Top Line Revenue	A1				
Pass Through Revenue	A2				
Real Revenue	A3	100%	100%		
Profit	A4	B4	C4	D4	E4
Owner's Comp	A5	B5	C5	D5	E5
Owner's Tax	A6	B6	C6	D6	E6
Operating Expenses	A7	B7	C7	D7	E7
Repairs, Vacancy, Turnover	A8	B8	C8	D8	E8

will always be paying property taxes and insurance on your properties.

Sources:

P (Principal) = balance sheet under liabilities (the payments made to pay down the principal)

I (Interest) = Profit and loss

T (Taxes) = Profit and loss

I (Insurance) = Profit and loss

Quick hack for total PITI = spreadsheet detailing all PITI payments that you pay in a month

A3: Real Revenue (actual dollar amount)

This cell is very simple. It's the Top Line Revenue *minus* the PITI.

This is the money that is available to allocate to your Profit First accounts.

Formula:

$$\begin{array}{rl} & \text{TOP LINE REVENUE} \\ - & \underline{\text{PITI}} \\ = & \text{REAL REVENUE} \\ & \text{(or: A1 – A2 = A3)} \end{array}$$

A4: Profit (actual dollar amount)

This is the amount of cash you have left over after paying all your PITI, expenses, owner's comp, and owner's taxes. If you're currently running Profit First, this would include the money you've saved in the **Profit** account.

Formula:

REAL REVENUE
- OWNER'S COMP
- OWNER'S TAX
- OPERATING EXPENSES
- REPAIRS, TURNOVER, VACANCY
= PROFIT

(or: A3 – A5 – A6 – A7 – A8 = A4)

A5: Owner's Comp (actual dollar amount)

This is exactly like a selling company. It's what you took out of the business for yourself. Owners (including you) pay themselves in many ways. Here are some common ways to look for how you may have paid yourself.

- Owner's Draws/Disbursements
- Payroll
- Reimbursements

Sources:

Owner's Draws/Disbursements = Balance sheet

Payroll = Profit and loss

Reimbursements = Profit and loss statement

A6: Owner's Tax (actual dollar amount)

This is the amount you paid or set aside for your business taxes or your personal taxes.

This money is for the IRS. It is the amount of tax money:

- Your entity *already* paid for business and/or owner taxes.
- Your entity set aside in the **Owner's Tax** account to pay your business and/or owner taxes.

This is *not* the property taxes related to holding your rental properties. That will be in PITI.

Source: Profit and loss—more than likely there won't be any entries because the business hasn't paid your taxes before.

A7: Operating Expenses (actual dollar amount)

"Cost to run the business and office"

Operating Expenses = OpEx

Catch-all for all business expenses that are not related to you making money.

This number does *not* include the principal, interest, property taxes, and insurance related to your rentals. OpEx does not include

- PITI
- Owner's Comp
- Owner's Tax
- Repairs, vacancy, and turnover

Source: Expenses = Profit and loss

A8: Repairs, Vacancy, and Turnover (actual dollar amount)

We track these amounts specifically because these are usually built into your upfront formula for how a rental property will cash flow and are usually the biggest expenses you will have in a rental business. Put the actual dollar amount you have spent over the last year tied to repairs, vacancy, and turnover.

Source: Repairs, vacancy, and turnover = profit and loss

B4 – B8: Current Percentages

Every cell here is a simple formula to get the percentages you are operating on currently. You will be dividing the actual dollar amounts for the accounts by the Real Revenue number.

$$B4 = A4 \div A3$$
$$B5 = A5 \div A3$$
$$B6 = A6 \div A3$$
$$B7 = A7 \div A3$$
$$B8 = A8 \div A3$$

These percentages will immediately be able to tell you whether you are way off track as a business.

C4 – C8: PF % = the TAPs

These cells are going to be the TAPs based on your Real Revenue for a year. Refer to the Rental Company

RENTAL COMPANY TAPS

	A	B	C	D	E	F
Annual Real Revenue Range	$0–$250K	$250–$500K	$500K–$1M	$1M–$5M	$5M–$10M	$10M–$50M
Real Revenue	100%	100%	100%	100%	100%	100%
Profit	10%	15%	20%	15%	20%	25%
Owner's Pay	40%	30%	15%	10%	5%	0%
Owner's Tax	5%	5%	5%	5%	5%	5%
Operating Expenses	30%	35%	45%	55%	55%	55%
Repairs, Vacancy, Turnover	15%	15%	15%	15%	15%	15%

TAPs table, pick the Column (A, B, C, and so on.) you fall into, and put those percentages in C4–C8.
Example: You have Real Revenue of $223,000 for the past year. Your cells would be:

C4 = 10%
C5 = 40%
C6 = 5%
C7 = 30%
C8 = 15%

You can now compare your actual percentages in cells B4–B8 to the TAPs in C4–C8 to see how close you are to being a healthy company.

D4 – D7: Profit First dollar amount

These cells are where you put the amounts that you should sock away into the respective accounts if you have been following Profit First. If you haven't implemented the system yet, they show you what you should have funded into accounts. These cells are a formula also. The Profit First Dollar Amounts are found by multiplying the Real Revenue by the TAPs.

Formula for getting the Profit First dollar amounts:

$D4 = A3 \times C4$
$D5 = A3 \times C5$
$D6 = A3 \times C6$
$D7 = A3 \times C7$
$D8 = A3 \times C8$

After inserting the formulas, you now have the Profit First dollar amounts for the accounts based on the Real Revenue and TAPs.

E4 – E7: The Difference

These cells tell you the difference between the dollar amounts you had in the first column *minus* what the Profit First dollar amounts should have been.

Here is the formula for getting the difference:

E4 = A4 – D4

E5 = A5 – D5

E6 = A6 – D6

E7 = A7 – D7

E8 = A8 – D8

If the number is negative, you need to up your actual number for that account. If the number is positive, you need to spend less or save less for that account.

ACKNOWLEDGMENTS

This book would not have been possible without a lot of great people in my life. A book is a massively big project to undertake, but it makes it so much better when you have key people in your life helping you.

First, I want to thank Mike Michalowicz. Mike is already changing the world with Profit First. Now we're changing the real estate investing world, and it all started with Mike's original book. I am very grateful for his friendship and mentorship during this process and want to thank him for being a genuinely nice person behind the scenes just as he is in the spotlight. I have learned so much and know I will learn more.

Another person who deserves as much thanks as Mike is AJ Harper. She guided me through her course, the Top Three Book Workshop, to focus on *you,* the reader, and make sure that every single line would benefit you. She also helped edit the book, for which I will be forever grateful, because editing is the bane of my existence. If you ever consider writing a book to change lives, please go to ajharper.com/top-three-book-workshop/ and sign up for her workshop. You will receive your money's worth and more.

My wife and daughter also deserve special recognition because without their love and support, I could never have done this book and spent countless hours on it early in the morning and at night. I am so grateful for my wife and my daughter and love them to death.

My parents have been supportive of anything I've ever done, and this project has been no different. I understand now at this age how incredibly blessed I've been to have the parents I do. A huge thank you to both of them for their love and support my whole life.

I also want to thank my in-laws, who are two of the best human beings I know. They constantly ask me about the book and my company and are genuinely interested in what we're doing with Profit First and the real estate world. Their support and encouragement have been huge.

A special thank you to Gary Harper of Sharper Business Solutions. He is the one who pushed me to get out years ago and start my own company helping real estate investors *and* he was the one who introduced me to the original Profit First book. I will be forever grateful to Gary.

A *huge* thank you to everyone who gave me their Profit First stories to be included in this book. It was so inspiring and humbling to hear how Profit First has changed so many investors' lives already.

Thank you to the people who provided feedback or gave endorsements for the book. It is a big time commitment to read a book and provide feedback, so I will be forever grateful.

Thank you to Dan Brault, who helped me see that some of my personal struggles should be in the book to help others with whatever they might be going through.

I want to thank the special people who are on the team at Simple CFO: Tim Jon, my operations manager who has helped with this book a lot. John Cruz is a virtual assistant whom I've worked with for more than six years. He's a dear personal friend and the hardest working person I know. Michael Hansen, who is our internal CFO, helped to clarify my message and work through Pass Through Revenue. Matt Siemer, Rocky Lalvani, Rebecca Howell, Christina Gutierrez, Diana Miret, Shari James, and Quincy Pierce are all on the front lines as CFOs in our business and they make a direct and profound impact on the companies with which they work.

Another *huge* thank you goes to the clients at Simple CFO. Thank you for putting your trust in us in order to help you know your numbers, get profitable, and find true financial peace and freedom. I appreciate every single one of you. This book is another way I wanted to provide value to you because you deserve all the value in the world.

I also want to thank *you*. Thank you for reading this book. Thank you for wanting to be different than so many other investors when it comes to their finances. Thank you for taking the time to read this section. Thank you for wanting to change your mindset, change your finances, and change your life. Thank you for being who you are and for starting your journey to happiness, peace, and greater profitability. Thank you for investing in yourself and for taking the plunge.

As you can see, I have had a *lot* of great people in my life. I would encourage you to write down a list of all the people that have invested in you. If that list is short, be very grateful for any name on that list. If that list is long, be grateful that you have so many good people in your life. I would not be here and this book would not be here without all of these great people. I am humbled to walk with giants and to learn from incredible people. I have been truly blessed and this book is a way to give back to anyone that has ever invested in me.

ABOUT THE AUTHOR

David Richter is an active real estate investor who helps other investors turn their failing businesses around, build cash reserves, and grow wealth. The founder of Simple CFO Solutions, LLC, his mission is to transform the real estate industry by helping real estate investors gain true financial clarity and freedom.

As a real estate investor, David has sat in every seat. He helped close more than 850 deals, including wholesale, turnkey, BRRRR, owner finance, rentals, lease options, and other exit strategies. He found his calling when, after helping a real estate business build from five to twenty-five deals a month, he discovered a passion for helping real estate investors keep the profits they earned. Connect with David at simplecfosolutions.com/pfrei.

CPSIA information can be obtained
at www.ICGtesting.com
Printed in the USA
LVHW090559101221
705823LV00002B/167

9 781737 514817